Addresses on

THE SECOND EPISTLE TO THE

CORINTHIANS

By H. A. IRONSIDE, Litt. D.

Expository Sermons Preached in the
MOODY MEMORIAL CHURCH, CHICAGO, ILL.

LOIZEAUX BROTHERS
Neptune, New Jersey

FIRST EDITION, JUNE 1939
FOURTEENTH PRINTING, MAY 1979

Published by LOIZEAUX BROTHERS, Inc.
*A Nonprofit Organization, Devoted to the Lord's Work
and to the Spread of His Truth*

ISBN 0-87213-355-9
PRINTED IN THE UNITED STATES OF AMERICA

CONTENTS

PREFATORY NOTE

Like the preceding volume of addresses on First Corinthians, these messages were given on Sunday mornings to the congregation of the Moody Memorial Church and to the many thousands comprising the Radio audience. My desire was to make them as clear, concise and simple as possible, so that the least instructed of my hearers might benefit by them. They were reported by Mrs. Arvilla Garner, to whom I am greatly indebted for her competent stenography.

H. A. IRONSIDE.

Chicago, 1939.

COMFORT IN AFFLICTION

✓ ✓ ✓

"Paul, an apostle of Jesus Christ by the will of God, and Timothy our brother, unto the church of God which is at Corinth, with all the saints which are in all Achaia: Grace be to you and peace from God our Father, and from the Lord Jesus Christ. Blessed be God, even the Father of our Lord Jesus Christ, the Father of mercies, and the God of all comfort; who comforteth us in all our tribulation, that we may be able to comfort them which are in any trouble, by the comfort wherewith we ourselves are comforted of God. For as the sufferings of Christ abound in us, so our consolation also aboundeth by Christ. And whether we be afflicted, it is for your consolation and salvation, which is effectual in the enduring of the same sufferings which we also suffer: or whether we be comforted, it is for your consolation and salvation. And our hope of you is stedfast, knowing, that as ye are partakers of the sufferings, so shall ye be also of the consolation" (2 Cor. 1: 1-7).

✓ ✓ ✓

THE first letter to the Corinthians, as we have seen,* has to do with order in the Church of God here on earth. Someone has aptly called it, "The Charter of the Church." There are some people who would foolishly set to

_____
* In "Addresses on First Corinthians," same author and publishers.

9

one side most of Paul's earlier epistles as though they did not have full dispensational place for our day, but it is an important thing to note that if we were to set First Corinthians to one side we would then have no other portion of the New Testament giving us any direction whatsoever as to the order and discipline of the churches of God here in the world. Here alone we get divine instruction as to these things.

When we come to the second epistle to the Corinthians, the apostle unfolds for us the ministry of the churches of God. I say "churches" because we are thinking of individual congregations. The two terms are used in Scripture. Paul says, "I persecuted the Church of God, and wasted it" (Gal. 1: 13). He means the entire Church wherever he found it, but he also speaks of the churches of God in Judea and in Galatia, etc., referring to local assemblies. God has Himself appointed the ministry for His churches, and we have the order and the choosing of that ministry, the nature of it, in this second letter to the Corinthians.

First of all we find that it is a divinely trained ministry. It is not a question of college training; it is not a question of graduating from a university nor of going through some particular seminary. All of these things may or may not be important in the training of a servant of God, but the first great pre-requisite is that Christ's minister be one who has learned to walk with the blessed Lord Jesus and to go through the school of affliction. At the beginning of the letter we read how wonderfully God sustains His servants in the hour of trial.

In this first chapter we have the apostolic salutation (vers. 1, 2): "Paul, an apostle (a sent one) of Jesus Christ by the will of God, and Timothy our brother, unto the church of God which is at Corinth, with all the saints which are in all Achaia." Achaia was the name of the district, or province, as we would call it today, and Corinth was its chief city. Paul had labored for a year and a half in Corinth, and through his labors a great many throughout the entire district of Achaia had been converted. A church of God had been formed in the city, a rather remarkable church in some ways because we read, "They came behind in no gift." Evidences of special divine favor rested upon them, and yet it was a church that, like others, had to endure trial and affliction for the testimony of Jesus Christ.

Paul wishes, "Grace and peace from God our Father, and from the Lord Jesus Christ," in view of trial. It is not the grace that saves that is spoken of here; they were already saved; it is the grace that sustains. We who are saved by grace still need fresh supplies of grace for every step of the way, and so we are bidden to "Come boldly unto the throne of grace, that we may obtain mercy, and find grace for seasonable help" (Heb. 4:16, N.T.). This is the grace which the apostle prays may be the abiding portion of the people of God. And then he asks that peace may be given. It is not peace *with* God. That they already enjoyed. Every rightly instructed believer ought to enter into that. "Being justified by faith, we have peace with God through our Lord Jesus Christ" (Rom. 5:1)—this is peace in view of the sin question. That has been settled and our consciences now are at peace, for we know that God is satisfied and we rest in that which has satisfied Him. But there is another aspect of peace that we need. We are going through a difficult scene, traveling through a world where affliction, sorrow, bereavement, and suffering abound, and if it were not for special mercy ministered to us from day to day we might be overwhelmed by the difficulties of our pilgrim journey. "Thou wilt keep him in perfect peace, whose mind is stayed on thee: because he trusteth in Thee" (Isa. 26:3). This is the peace for which the apostle prays, that the people of God may so walk before Him that they may enjoy His peace whatever their circumstances. As we read in Philippians 4:6, "Be not anxious about anything; but in everything by prayer and suppli-

cation with thanksgiving let your requests be
made known unto God."

In the early days of the Church when thousands
were sealing their testimony with their blood,
God enabled His beloved people to go through the
keenest sufferings not only without resentment
toward their enemies, but with the peace of God
garrisoning their hearts, and He still calls on
people to give up their lives for the gospel's sake.
The noble army of martyrs praise Him. Christianity is a wonderful thing; it enables people to
triumph over all circumstances. As we think of
what some of the missionaries of the cross are
called upon to endure, it ought to make many of
us at home ashamed that we allow such trivial
things to disturb our spirits. "Ye have not yet
resisted unto blood, striving against sin" (Heb.
12: 4). Think of the little things that fret us
because we are a bit short of money now and
then, because we have pain and aches occasionally,
because we have to face a little in the way
of trouble and trial. How small these things are
compared with what many of God's dear servants
in distant places are undergoing for Him! But
the same grace that sustains them in their trial
is needed to sustain us in ours, and, thank God,
it is at our disposal. The apostle celebrates that
grace in the verses that follow.

First, there is an overflowing of the heart in

praise. "Blessed be God." Does your heart often say that? Let the Lord be praised! Let Him be worshiped and adored! How much there is to praise Him for. "Blessed be God!" Billy Bray, the Cornish miner, used to say, "If they were to put me in a barrel, I would shout, 'Glory to God!' through the bung-hole." When poverty stared him in the face, he said, "If the meal barrel is empty, I will put my head in the barrel and praise the Lord." One day his wife came to him and said, "Do you know, we haven't a penny left?"

"Is that so?" he said.

"And what is more, we have no food left. I went to the barrel to see whether I could find something to do a little baking with, but there is nothing left. Now practise what you preach, and put your head in the flour-barrel and say, 'Praise the Lord.' "

He said, "Well, if you will put yours in with me, I will."

"All right," she said; "I will."

And so they went to the empty flour-barrel and both put their heads in and said, "Praise the Lord!" and then they prayed. When they came out, there was a lot of flour on their heads, they were pretty well powdered-up. They went into the study with a song of joy in their hearts, and almost the next thing there was a knock at the door, and some one said that the Lord had sent

him to minister to them. It is a great thing to
be able to bless the Lord whatever our circumstances are.

David says, "I will bless the Lord at all times:
His praise shall continually be in my mouth"
(Ps. 34: 1). I am afraid some of us do not know
much about that. We bless the Lord when we
have plenty, and growl when we have not. But
David says, "I will bless the Lord at *all* times."
Job was able to say, "The Lord gave, and the
Lord hath taken away; blessed be the name of the
Lord" (Job 1: 21). You know the devil said to
God, "That man loves You only for what he gets
out of You; he loves You for the gifts You give
him." So God said, "Take everything away, and
see." And Satan took everything away, and Job
says, "Bless the Lord anyway!" God grant that
He may fill our hearts with praise! "Whoso
offereth praise glorifieth Me." Think of that the
next time you feel like growling and complaining.

"Blessed be God!" And who is this God that
we bless? "Even the Father of our Lord Jesus
Christ." Notice, He does not here suggest His
Fatherhood of us as believers. That comes out
later, but first of all He is the Father of our Lord
Jesus Christ. You see our blessed Lord is His
Son by a unique relationship into which no one
else can ever enter. We are sons of God by a
second birth, but our Lord Jesus Christ is the

Son of God from all eternity, and therefore in a special sense God is the Father of our Lord Jesus Christ. Here then is the proof of His love. He had but the one Son and He gave Him for us, and shall we ever doubt His love because times seem a little difficult, sickness lays us low, finances seem to disappear, bereavement enters our home? "He that spared not His own Son, but delivered Him up for us all, how shall He not with Him also freely give us all things?" (Rom. 8: 32). "Blessed be God, even the Father of our Lord Jesus Christ."

And then notice the next title Paul gives Him, "The Father of mercies." That is, our God is the source of every mercy that comes to us. David says, "Goodness and mercy shall follow me all the days of my life: and I will dwell in the house of the Lord for ever" (Ps. 23: 6). Some of these mercies we do not always appreciate. We sometimes think perhaps that God is dealing hardly with us when He is really dealing with us in mercy. A friend of mine who went to Heaven some years ago, told of a time when he was riding on the top of an omnibus in Vienna, Austria, and they were held up because a flock of sheep was going down the street. As the folk on the bus leaned over to see what was going on, they noticed that there were two dogs running hither and thither to keep the sheep in the way. This friend turned to a stranger seated beside him and said, "Do you know the names of those two dogs?"

The man said, "Indeed, I do not; I have never seen a sight like this before."

"Well," said my friend, "I think I know their names."

"Do you?"

"Yes; one of them is 'Goodness' and the other is 'Mercy,' for David wrote about goodness and mercy following him all the days of his life."

You might not think it was goodness and mercy to have a couple of dogs yapping at you to keep you from going to the left or to the right, but it is God's mercy that keeps us in the straight and narrow way, and He uses trial and difficulty for that very purpose. He is "the Father of mercies."

And then again He is called "The God of all comfort." There are two things of which God is said to have the monopoly: He is "the God of *all* grace" and He is "the God of *all* comfort." All grace comes from Him, all lasting comfort comes from Him. "Consolation" and "comfort" are the same in the original text, and you get it from God. I suppose you have noticed that in the Word of God the three Persons of the blessed adorable Trinity are all spoken of as engaged in the ministry of comfort. Here we have the Father of our Lord Jesus Christ as the God of all comfort. Then we remember the title the blessed Lord uses for the Holy Spirit. John 14, 15 and 16 speak of Him as "Another Comforter," the *"Parakletos,"* the One who comes to our help to sustain and strengthen. And in 1 John 2: 1 we read, "If any man sin, we have an *Advocate* with the Father, Jesus Christ the righteous." The word "Advocate" is the same Greek word translated "Comforter" in the other passages. "If any man sin, we have a Comforter." That refers to the Lord Jesus. So God the Father is the Comforter, God the Holy Ghost is the Comforter, and God the Son is the Comforter. How wonderfully well we are taken care of! The entire Godhead is engaged in comforting and sustaining the people of the Lord.

The first aspect of comfort we all need is that of forgiveness. It was the Lord Jesus who said to the poor troubled one, "Daughter, be of good comfort; thy faith hath made thee whole" (Matt. 9: 22). Has He said that to you? Do you know the comfort of divine forgiveness? "Comfort ye, comfort ye My people...cry unto her... that her iniquity is pardoned: for she hath received of the Lord's hand double for all her sins" (Isa. 40: 1, 2). The "double" was really the doubling up of the bond after it was paid, and the debt that stood against us has been paid by our Lord Jesus, and so ours may be the comfort of forgiveness.

But then we need comfort to help in every time
of trial as we go through this world, and we
have the blessed Holy Spirit dwelling within us
to be our Comforter.   There is a lovely word in
the sixty-sixth chapter of the book of the Prophet
Isaiah, "As one whom his mother comforteth, so
will I comfort you."   There are different Hebrew
words translated "comfort."   This particular
one really comes from a root that means "to
sigh."   "As one whom his mother sighs with, so
I the Lord will sigh with you."   Why did they
translate that "comfort"?   Do you get any comfort like that?   Do you remember when you were
a little tot and in some trouble and distress, and
mother drew you into her arms and patted your
head and said, "Yes, yes, mother understands;
mother feels with you in it all"?   Your mother
"sighed" with you, and it helped wonderfully.
Mothers are wonderful people.   I sometimes say
they are amiable witches, they are wonder-
workers.   A little chap running around the yard
hurts himself, the knee is cut, and mother picks
him up in her arms, and even before she gets the
mercurochrome she kisses it and says, "Yes, yes,
mother knows it hurts," and the little fellow says,
"Mamma, it is better already."   Our God enters
with us into all our troubles; He is not an in-
different spectator.

A minister tells the story how years ago when

he was a young preacher he had been very busy
one entire week and did not have time to get at
his Sunday sermons until Saturday morning. He
felt he must take the entire day to concentrate
and get ready for the Lord's Day services. He
said to his wife, "My dear, I must not be dis-
turbed this morning. I am going into my study
and have to get up two sermons for tomorrow.
You just tell everybody I cannot see them." And
so she took her place as guardian. She had not
been told to keep the children out, and the little
folks came in and were playing noisily. Finally
he said, "Mother, I cannot study with these children making so much noise," and so she came
running with a wooden basin full of nuts and a
nut-cracker, thinking that would keep them
occupied. But there was only one nut-cracker
and there were three children, and they soon
began fussing about who should have it. The
little girl found she could crack nuts without a
cracker; she could go to the door and put the
nut against the jamb and pull the door and the
nut was cracked. And so she held the nuts while
her brother pulled the door, but suddenly the
door came too quickly and she did not get her
finger away, and she let out such a scream that
the poor man with his overwrought nerves
jumped up and said, "Mother, mother, you must
come and take these noisy children away. I can-

not study with them here." She came running
along and said, "Come, you must come away," and
started down the hallway with them. The little
thing was crying so hard, and the minister could
hear the mother saying, "Oh, my darling, does it
hurt so much? Does it hurt so dreadfully?" And
between her sobs she said, "It isn't that it hurts
so much, but Daddy never even said, 'Oh'!" To
feel there was no loving sympathy was what hurt.

Dear child of God, am I speaking to some one
lying on a bed of sickness, enduring pain and
anguish?* Do you love the Lord Jesus? He loves
you, and your God and Father is looking down
upon you and saying, "Oh". For it is written,
"In all their affliction He was afflicted, and the
angel of His presence saved them: in His love
and in His pity he redeemed them" (Isa. 63: 9).
As one whom his mother says "Oh" with, so the
Lord your God says "Oh" with you. His comfort
is a very real thing. He feels for you, and it is
said of the Lord Jesus, "We have not an high
priest which cannot be touched with the feeling
of our infirmities; but was in all points tempted
like as we are, apart from sin" (Heb. 2:15, N.T.).
He has been over the road. You can never suffer
as He did; He sounded the depths of human lone-

---

*These messages were broadcast over the Radio as well
as addressed to the audience in the church auditorium.

liness and anguish, and now He can feel for you
in all you go through.

And so the apostle says, "Who comforteth us
in all our tribulation, that we may be able to
comfort them which are in any trouble, by the
comfort wherewith we ourselves are comforted
of God." We are often so selfish. We want
people to take cognizance of our suffering; we
want sympathy and a kind word and love. But
we forget that there are others all around us who
need it too, and if God comforts you in your trial,
it is that you may comfort some one else. You
will be able to say, "I know; I have been through
it myself, and let me tell you how wonderfully
the Lord undertook for me. He can do it for
you too."

"For as the sufferings of Christ abound in us,
so our consolation also aboundeth by Christ."
The greater the suffering, the more we are called
upon to endure, the more wonderful the opportunity we have of learning what a God our God
is, and how marvelously He can meet every need
of the human heart.

"Whether we be afflicted," says the apostle, "it
is for your consolation and salvation." He was
willing to suffer that others might be blessed.
"Which is effectual in the enduring of the same
sufferings which we also suffer." Since you

Corinthians became Christians you are suffering for Christ. We suffered to bring Christ to you, and you are now entering into what we have been enduring. Let us together find our comfort in God.

"Whether we be comforted, it is for your consolation and salvation. And our hope of you is stedfast, knowing, that as ye are partakers of the sufferings, so shall ye be also of the consolation." What a word of cheer that ought to be to any tried, troubled saint of God. You are partaker of the suffering, you are going through a time of special stress, but according to the Word of God you shall be partaker of the consolation. The Lord is ready to undertake for you, He in His infinite grace is waiting to minister to your deep need. Just trust Him, and after that you have suffered a while He will bring you out to His own praise and glory. Meanwhile may it be yours and mine to "glorify Him in the fire."

If you are unsaved, how much you are missing! You do not know the comfort of the Triune God. You are turning away from your best Friend, and you do not realize it. You remember the invitation of the Lord Jesus as He looked out upon the sin-sick world and said, "Come unto Me, all ye that labor and are heavy laden, and I will give you rest" (Matt. 11: 28). And this invitation comes to you today. Will you come? Will you find in Him that rest which you can never find anywhere else? No matter what your sin, no matter what your anxiety, He waits to meet every need if you will only trust Him.

THREEFOLD DELIVERANCE

1 1 1

"For we would not, brethren, have you ignorant of our
trouble which came to us in Asia, that we were pressed out
of measure, above strength, insomuch that we despaired
even of life: but we had the sentence of death in ourselves,
that we should not trust in ourselves, but in God which
raiseth the dead: who delivered us from so great a death,
and doth deliver: in whom we trust that He will yet deliver
us; ye also helping together by prayer for us, that for the
gift bestowed upon us by the means of many persons thanks
may be given by many on our behalf. For our rejoicing
is this, the testimony of our conscience, that in simplicity
and godly sincerity, not with fleshly wisdom, but by the
grace of God, we have had our conversation in the world,
and more abundantly to you-ward. For we write none other
things unto you, than what ye read or acknowledge; and I
trust ye shall acknowledge even to the end; as also ye have
acknowledged us in part, that we are your rejoicing, even
as ye also are ours in the day of the Lord Jesus. And in
this confidence I was minded to come unto you before, that
ye might have a second benefit; and to pass by you into
Macedonia, and to come again out of Macedonia unto you,
and of you to be brought on my way toward Judæa. When
I therefore was thus minded, did I use lightness? or the
things that I purpose, do I purpose according to the flesh,
that with me there should be yea yea, and nay nay? But
as God is true, our word toward you was not yea and nay.
For the Son of God, Jesus Christ, who was preached among
you by us, even by me and Silvanus and Timotheus, was
not yea and nay, but in Him was yea. For all the promises
of God in Him are yea, and in Him Amen, uhto the glory
of God by us" (2 Cor. 1: 8-20).

BEFORE continuing the exposition of this book it may be well to give a brief outline of its contents. In chapters 1 to 7 the apostle dwells in large measure on the trials, the character, and the training of the servant of Christ, and the result of his ministry. He uses himself largely as an example in order to bring these things home to us.

In chapters 8 and 9 we have the second division of this epistle, in which the apostle deals with a question that comes home to every one of us, our money. In other words, the subject is, "The Grace of Giving." Giving is a grace. The natural man wants to get rather than to give. Here and there we run across generous folk who, even in their unconverted days, get a certain satisfaction out of giving to others, but most of us like to get, to receive rather than to distribute. But when Christ works in the soul, giving to those in need and for the furtherance of the work of the Lord becomes the joy of life. And so we speak of the Grace of Giving, and this subject is taken up very fully in these chapters.

In chapters 10 to 12, the third division of the epistle, we have Paul's vindication of his own apostleship. There were those dogging his steps, moving in and out among his converts, reflecting upon his ministry and calling in question his apostolic authority. And so he found it necessary, under the guidance of the Spirit of God, to insist upon the fact that he was actually an apostle of the Lord Jesus Christ. Chapter 13 is the conclusion.

This gives us the outline of the epistle, and with this before us we turn to consider the verses of the second section of this first chapter. Here we read of the troubles, the difficulties, the perplexities that Paul and his fellow-laborers were going through, but he shows that God has a wonderful purpose in permitting all these things. It is hard for us to realize, but it is true that God can do far more with a broken man than with a man who seems strong in his own strength and power. And so He permits trouble to come upon His people, and even upon His chosen vessels, in order that they may be humble and broken in spirit before Him.

Our Lord Jesus said, "Blessed are the poor in spirit: for theirs is the kingdom of heaven" (Matt. 5:3). We naturally admire a man of strength and initiative, a man who has a great deal of self-confidence and self-esteem. It was our great President Theodore Roosevelt who said, "I hate a meek man." I am sure he did not realize the implication that might be taken from that statement, for that would imply hatred of our Lord Jesus Christ, which we know he never meant. "Take My yoke upon you, and learn of

Me; for I am meek and lowly in heart: and ye shall find rest unto your souls" (Matt. 11:29). We do not come naturally by meekness. In the prophecy of Zephaniah (2:3) we are admonished to "seek meekness," as though it is a very rare jewel of character which is found only by careful searching. It is not like us to seek meekness; as a rule we are naturally so proud, we are so haughty, so wickedly conceited, so self-occupied. Because of these very things if God is going to use us in His service, He has to permit us to go through experiences which will humble and break us.

We are told how Goldsmidt sat listening to Jenny Lind as she charmed thousands by her wonderful voice. Some one asked the great music critic, "What do you think of her? Isn't she marvelous?"

"Well," he said, "she is wonderful; she needs just one thing; she needs to have her heart broken. If her heart were broken, she would be the greatest singer in the world."

Afterward, you remember, he won her heart and then broke it by his unkindness, and after that there was a depth of tenderness, there was something to her singing that stirred people as nothing else had ever done in the past. So it is with preachers of the Word of God. If they stand apart from the troubles that others are going through, they will have no real message for the hearts of men. It is the man who in some measure at least is like his Master, "A Man of sorrows and acquainted with grief," who is able to minister to a broken-hearted, suffering, distressed people. And so the apostle Paul learned to glory in tribulation and to thank God for distresses because they only fitted him the better to be a servant of Him of whom it is written, "In all their affliction He was afflicted, and the angel of His presence saved them" (Isa. 63: 9).

Listen again to these words, "For we would not, brethren, have you ignorant of our trouble which came to us in Asia, that we were pressed out of measure, above strength, insomuch that we despaired even of life." When that great raging crowd gathered about him, howling for his life, and would have trampled him beneath their feet, and he saw nothing but a martyr's death before him, nevertheless Paul says, "We had the sentence of death in ourselves, that we should not trust in ourselves, but in God which raiseth the dead." Paul could face that howling mob and say, "It is all right if they tear us to pieces, if they tear us limb from limb. If they utterly destroy this mortal body, it means nothing to us. We have already taken the place of death with Christ, we have already said that we are dead to the world, to its favor, and to its follies, and now if they make that actually true by destroying these bodies, it is all right. We have the sentence of death in ourselves, we are men devoted to death, men who have made a rendezvous with death for Jesus' sake. Our trust is in Him who raiseth the dead, even the living God." It is only as a man knows the power of Christ working within him that he is able to speak like this, and to live it out, but this is what has enabled the people of God to triumph all down through the centuries. Again and again the devil has stirred up hatred against Christ's servants, and the martyrs are numbered by the thousands and tens of thousands, but Satan has been foiled every time that he has tried to hinder the work of the Lord by persecution. Still the blood of the martyrs is the seed of the Church. The gospel flourishes in times of tribulation.

The Church's worst times are not times of suffering, of martyrdom. The Church's most dangerous periods are those when she is enjoying the patronage of the world. The Church is never in such grave danger as when the world is fawning upon it, when worldlings look upon it with favor. Our Lord Jesus warned His disciples of the danger when all men spake well of them. When people are persecuted for Christ's sake, when they have to go through affliction and troubles and sorrows, that is the time they draw nearer to the Lord. You remember the old fable in our school-books, how the sun and the wind were trying to see which was the stronger. The traveler went on his way and each tried to see which could get him to take his overcoat off first. The wind blew and blew, but the traveler wrapped his coat about him more securely. And then the sun beamed upon the man and he began to perspire, and off went the coat. It is when worldly prosperity shines upon the Church that off goes the robe of righteous behavior. But when the wintry blasts of trouble and persecution break upon it, then the Church wraps itself all the more closely in the garment of salvation. Paul knew that tribulation was for blessing. God uses broken men, and if men will not humble themselves before Him in order to make them vessels to carry His testimony to others, He will give them experiences to break them.

Then, observe, the apostle found that despite the persecution God came in at the right moment with a threefold deliverance. In verse 10 we read: "Who delivered us from so great a death, and doth deliver: in whom we trust that He will yet deliver us." We can apply this to the question of our salvation. Actually the apostle is speaking of deliverance from trial and distress here on the earth. God has delivered, and as we continue our service God does deliver, and as we look forward to the future He will yet deliver. This is faith's confidence in our gracious God and Father.

But we may apply it spiritually. Our salvation, in a spiritual sense, is threefold, and we may read it: "Who saved us from so great a death, and doth save: in whom we trust that He will yet save us." When we came to Him as poor lost sinners, He saved us from the judgment due to our sins. How great a death was that from which we were delivered. And day by day as we go through this scene "He doth deliver us." He delivers from the power of sin, from the strength of our own natures. He delivers from temptation; He, always with the temptation, makes "a way of escape that ye may be able to bear it" (1 Cor. 10:13). And one of these days, at the coming of our Lord Jesus Christ and our gathering together unto Him, our salvation will be completed. And so we look on to that time when "He shall yet deliver," when He will fully and completely save us. We have often put it like this: He has saved us from the judgment due to sin and from the guilt of sin; He does save us from the power of sin; by and by He will save us from the very presence of sin, giving us our glorified bodies when we will no longer have the least tendency to evil of any kind.

"Soon we'll pass this desert dreary,
    Soon we'll bid farewell to pain;
Nevermore be sad or weary,
    Never, never sin again."

What a deliverance that will be! When we will
never have to bow the knee again to say, "Forgive us our trespasses as we forgive others,"
when we will never have to wipe away tears of
penitence, for throughout endless ages we shall be
free from the presence of sin in the joy of everlasting communion with our blessed Lord. That
will be our complete deliverance, but meantime,
as we are going on, we tread the pilgrim way, and
need daily deliverance.

There are certain things that God has ordained
to be of assistance along the way. One of them
is mentioned in the eleventh verse: "Ye also helping together by prayer for us, that for the gift
bestowed upon us by the means of many persons
thanks may be given by many on our behalf."
Pray one for another. Those of us trying to
preach the Word, seeking to do public service for
the Lord Jesus Christ, will never know until we
get home to Heaven how much we are indebted
for sustaining grace to the prayers of God's hidden ones. My heart always rejoices when anyone
writes or says to me, "I am praying for you," for
I need to be prayed for. I am so forgetful about
prayer myself; so many times when I should be

praying I am busy at something else, and often if there is any power at all in my messages I know it is because somebody at home or in the audience is praying for me. One owes so much to the prayers of God's beloved people. Was there ever such a man of God as the apostle Paul in all the centuries since? And yet how dependent he was upon the prayers of believers. Go through his epistles and you will find again and again the exhortation, "Brethren, pray for us." Time spent in praying for the servants of God is not a waste of time or breath. Prayer accomplishes things for God, and God will do in answer to prayer what He will not do apart from prayer.

And so the apostle says, "Ye also helping together by prayer for us, that for the gift bestowed upon us by the means of many persons thanks may be given by many on our behalf." That is, we go out to preach the Word and God uses it in blessing, but we know it is not of ourselves; there are many persons backing us up, and praying and bearing up our ministry before God.

But now the man who would count on the sustaining power of the Spirit of God in the hour of trial, and the man who has a right to ask the saints of God to pray for him, is the man who can say what Paul said, in verse 12: "For our rejoicing is this, the testimony of our conscience, that in simplicity and godly sincerity, not with fleshly wisdom, but by the grace of God, we have had our behavior in the world, and more abundantly to you-ward." What a statement this is! Think of being able to turn to a group among whom he has ministered and say, "We have sought to be right; we have not given ourselves to any mere oratorical clap-trap when we have stood up to preach the Word, but we have done it in simplicity and godly sincerity, in genuineness in the sight of God." Is it not strange that we can be so particular as to how we appear in the sight of men, and yet can be so unreal in the presence of God? Think of even trying to preach the Word and, as far as man can see, putting one's whole soul into the effort to glorify Christ, and yet have hidden in the heart only the desire for the applause of men.

Paul could say, Our own conscience bears witness to the fact that we have tried to be real in the presence of God. And as we have ministered the Word we have sought to be honest with God as well as with man, not with fleshly wisdom, not depending upon the things that will reach the mere natural man and please and satisfy his craving for eloquence or excitement, but as acting in the fear of God we have had our behavior in the world. We have lived what we preached. We have not taught people to be honest and then been

dishonest ourselves. We have not called on people to be humble when we ourselves were proud.
We have not exhorted others to be self-denying
while we were grasping and covetous. We have
not told people that they ought to be unworldly
while we ourselves were going after the pleasures
and follies of the world. There is something here
to search our hearts, something to lead us into
the presence of God in self-judgment. Would to
God we could say what Paul says, "We have had
our behavior in the world in all integrity."

"For we write none other things unto you, than
what ye read or acknowledge; and I trust ye
shall acknowledge even to the end." He knew
that they were glad to recognize the fact that
they had been blessed through him, but on the
other hand they were being misled by people coming in and seeking to turn them away from their
first confidence in this man of God.

"We are your rejoicing, even as ye also are
ours in the day of the Lord Jesus." When by
and by we stand at the judgment-seat of Christ,
it will all be revealed. We led you to Christ, you
went on with God, and so brought joy to us. But
on the other hand, he knew that they were being
estranged by little gossipy things that were being
said by enemies of the truth, trying to alienate
the hearts of the Corinthians from Paul, and so
in the last part of this section he has to justify
himself.

He first tells them that he meant to come to them. He had never gotten there, and some evil people had taken that up and said, "Don't you see, he never meant to go; he is afraid to go. He writes pretty strong letters when he is away from you, his writing is strong, but his bodily presence is weak and his speech contemptible. He doesn't dare face you about these things. He just says he will go and then when it comes to doing it, he says, 'I will not go.' " But Paul declares that his purpose was "to pass by you into Macedonia, and to come again out of Macedonia unto you, and of you to be brought on my way toward Judæa." Corinth was a port, and he had to go from Corinth up to Macedonia, and while he had intended taking that trip certain circumstances had obliged him to take another route. Then he says, "When I therefore was thus minded, did I use lightness? or the things that I purpose, do I purpose according to the flesh, that with me there should be yea yea, and nay nay?" In other words, Did I have no real purpose?

Thus they wanted to accuse the apostle of lightness and carnality even in making appointments. He says, "As God is true, our word toward you was not yea and nay." It was not that he was careless or light or frivolous about it, but he was not able to carry out his plans because of certain providential happenings. Paul was a fol-

lower of the Lord Jesus Christ, and He did not
say one thing and mean another. "For the Son
of God, Jesus Christ, who was preached among
you by us, even by me and Silvanus and Timotheus, was not yea and nay, but in Him was yea."
See how he links others with himself. There is
something truly fine about a man who can always
recognize the greatness of other folk. Here Paul
links with him Silvanus and Timotheus. He says,
" We really intended to carry this out, but we
could not."

"For all the promises of God in Him are yea,
and in Him, Amen, unto the glory of God by us."
God never undertakes to do something He cannot
carry out. When He makes a promise, He will
always carry it through. He has never made a
promise to us that He will ever have to explain
away afterwards. He will never say, "I meant
to do that, but circumstances would not permit."
We have to make confessions like that from time
to time, but God never fails to keep His promises.
He is able to perform every one, and Christ is
the Amen to every promise of God.

OPERATIONS OF THE HOLY SPIRIT

✓ ✓ ✓

"Now He which stablisheth us with you in Christ, and hath anointed us, is God; who hath also sealed us, and given the earnest of the Spirit in our hearts" (2 Cor. 1: 21, 22).

✓ ✓ ✓

WE have in these verses, suggested at least, every operation of the Holy Spirit of God that is brought before us elsewhere in the New Testament. There is absolutely no ministry of the Holy Spirit as far as the believer is concerned that is not touched on here. In the Revised Version there is a slight change which helps to make it clearer. "Now He which *establisheth* us with you *into* Christ, and hath anointed us, is God."

When we think of establishment into Christ by the Holy Spirit, we necessarily think, if we are intelligent in the understanding of the truth of Scripture, of three very definite operations of the Holy Spirit. We think first of all of conviction, or sanctification by the Spirit. Secondly, we think of the new birth by the Spirit through the

Word. And thirdly, we think of the baptism of the Holy Spirit. All these operations are involved in the establishment of a believer into Christ. No one is in Christ by natural birth.

"As in Adam all die, even so in Christ shall all be made alive" (1 Cor. 15:22). All men naturally are in Adam. To be in Adam means that we have received life from Adam. He was our federal head; we belong by nature to Adam's race, and that entire race is under judgment because of sin. To be in Christ means that we have received life from Christ, and that He, the risen exalted One in heaven, is the Head of a new race, a new creation to which we now belong. The steps by which we enter into that new creation are laid down very clearly in the Word.

First of all, no one would ever come to Christ if it were not for the convicting, sanctifying work of the Holy Spirit of God. Unless the Spirit of God awakens a man, unless the Spirit of God brings him to see his lost condition, convicts him of the tremendous truths of Holy Scripture, no man would ever of himself turn to Christ. That is a very solemn fact, but it is a fact nevertheless. "It is not of him that willeth, nor of him that runneth, but of God that showeth mercy" (Rom. 9:16). On the other hand, it is quite possible for the Spirit of God to operate in convicting power on the heart of man and yet that man do

what the Jews did in Stephen's day. It is written
of them, "Ye do always resist the Holy Ghost"
(Acts 7: 51). So it is possible to be convicted
by the Spirit and yet to resist the Spirit. But
there must be the convicting work of the Spirit
of God or no one would ever come to Christ. Jesus
Christ said, "Nevertheless I tell you the truth; It
is expedient for you that I go away; for if I
go not away, the Comforter will not come unto
you; but if I depart, I will send Him unto you.
And when He is come, He will convince (or convict) the world of sin, and of righteousness, and
of judgment" (John 16: 7, 8). Conviction is far
more than a mere emotional breakdown. People
often confound conviction with that. Such a
breakdown may be there, and we are glad sometimes when it is. Most of us are so cold and
stony-hearted that it is refreshing to see people
break down and weep over their sins. The saintly
Rutherford complained in his day that there were
so few who ever had a sick night for sin. There
must be first a recognition of one's utterly lost
condition. The Spirit of God has come to convict
of sin, of righteousness, and of judgment. Our
Lord Jesus says, "Of sin, because they believe not
on Me." The great damning sin that is sending
men down to perdition is the rejection of the Lord
Jesus Christ. We are not told that the Spirit of
God was sent particularly to convict men of sins

of the flesh and sins of a general character. Every man's conscience convicts him of the sinfulness of licentiousness, of immoral living, of lying, of drunkenness, of pride and vanity, and all these other things, and if a man's conscience should be so dulled by continual sinning that it seems to cease to register, still there is God's holy law with its stern "thou shalts" and "thou shalt nots" which will convict any honest man of the sinfulness of a wicked life.

The Holy Spirit came to convict of the sin of rejecting the Lord Jesus Christ. God took the entire sin question into account when the Lord Jesus Christ hung on Calvary's cross, and because of what Christ did then and there, God is able to "be just and the Justifier of him which believeth in Jesus" (Rom. 3:26). But if men reject the Lord Jesus Christ, if men refuse to put their trust in Him, they have to go on to judgment, to face their own sins when they will be judged, every man according to his works. Some men rather pride themselves on their morality, on their respectability, and say, "I do not know that I need the salvation of God. I have never been guilty of breaking the moral code." Let me ask you this: Have you received the Lord Jesus Christ, God's blessed Son, as your own personal Saviour? If not, if you are still rejecting Him, you are guilty of the worst sin that any one can possibly commit, for God has given Heaven's best, in sending His blessed Son to earth to bleed and die for your redemption. Can there be any greater sin, any worse offense in the eyes of a holy God, than to reject that Saviour, to trample on His grace, and spurn His loving-kindness? It is the work of the Spirit of God to convict men of the sin of the rejection of Christ, and then to convict of righteousness. That is, to show men that though they have no righteousness of their own God has provided one for them in His risen Son. And so the apostle cries, "I would be found in Him, not having mine own righteousness, which is of the law, but that which is through the faith of Christ, the righteousness which is of God by faith" (Phil. 3:9). Yet Saul of Tarsus did not feel that way in his unconverted days. It was not until the Spirit of God convicted him of righteousness that he said, "Now I see it. I gladly part with every pretension to righteousness of my own; I would be found in Christ."

The Holy Spirit comes to convict of judgment. Not merely of judgment to come, but of the fact that this world is already under judgment, and that every believer is brought out from that judgment, and is raised up with this risen Christ, and so is called to walk apart from the world. Jesus said, "Because the prince of this world is judged" (John 16:11). Satan is the prince of this world,

and at the cross the ancient prophecy was fulfilled, "It shall bruise thy head, and thou shalt
bruise his heel" (Gen. 3: 15). At the cross Satan
bruised the heel of the Son of God, but there his
own head was bruised, and now he is a judged
prince, and the entire scene that recognizes his
authority is under judgment. You and I are
called by grace to step out from it all and take
our place with the Christ whom the world rejected.

Scripture sometimes uses another term for the
convicting work of the Spirit of God; it speaks
of the sanctification of the Spirit. In 1 Corinthians 6: 11 the apostle mentions some very ungodly
people, and then he says, "And such were some
of you: but ye are washed, but ye are sanctified,
but ye are justified in the name of the Lord Jesus,
and by the Spirit of our God."

Sanctification means to be set apart. You who
are in Christ, do you not remember when you
were part of this ungodly world? You lived for
the world and for self, and then the hour came
when earthly things began to pall upon you, you
lost your appetite for the pleasures of the world
and you were deeply concerned about your sinful
and lost condition. You said, "I cannot live like
this; I want something better than the world has
ever given me," and your trouble went on until
you came to Christ and believing in Him you

were justified. That was the sanctifying work of the Holy Spirit of God that thus led you to Christ. When people come to Christ, when the Spirit of God leads them to His blessed feet and they believe the gospel, what takes place? They are immediately born again. "Being born again," says Peter, "not of corruptible seed, but of incorruptible, by the Word of God, which liveth and abideth for ever" (1 Pet. 1: 23).

Our Lord Jesus said, "Except a man be born of water and of the Spirit, he cannot enter into the kingdom of God" (John 3: 5). People get confused about the water in that verse. They imagine sometimes that it means baptism, but Christian baptism had not been instituted when the Lord Jesus used those words. The best way to find out what it means is to go through John's writings and see how he speaks of water. You remember Jesus said to the woman at the well, "Whosoever drinketh of this water shall thirst again: but whosoever drinketh of the water that I shall give him shall never thirst: but the water that I shall give him shall be in him a well of water springing up into everlasting life." Whatever water means in John 3 it means exactly the same in John 4, and Jesus is not talking about drinking the water of baptism. Even when we are immersed we close our lips; we do not drink the water. But He is speaking of another kind of water altogether. We read in Revelation 22: 17: "Whosoever will, let him take of the water of life freely." What is the water of life? It is the offer of life that Jesus gives, the message that we have here in the Word of God. That Word has cleansing and refreshing power, and when we receive the Word in the simplicity of faith we are regenerated "by the washing of regeneration, and renewing of the Holy Ghost" (Titus 3:5). So then, the Spirit convicts, sanctifies, and regenerates through the Word, and more than that, the Spirit puts us into the Body of Christ.

"By one Spirit are we all baptized into one Body" (1 Cor. 12:12). Some time ago we were just so many units utterly uninterested in one another, but through grace we have been led not only to know that we are saved ourselves, but we have been brought into a blessed and hallowed unity with all fellow-believers. We are members of that one Body of which our Lord Jesus Christ is the Head. That is what it is to be established into Christ.

And then notice the next operation of the Spirit mentioned here: "And hath anointed us." The anointing is for service and illumination. You remember in Old Testament times three kinds of people were anointed with oil: prophets, priests, and kings; and oil is the recognized type of the

Holy Spirit. After His baptism in the Jordan, Jesus was anointed by God with the Holy Ghost and with power. When the Spirit of God descended upon Him in a special way, that was His anointing for His threefold office. He was Prophet on earth, He is Priest in Heaven, and He will be King when He comes again, and this blessed ministry is all in the power of the Holy Spirit. Though our Lord Jesus Christ was God, yet as to His Manhood He chose to do all His works in the Spirit's power, and so as believers we are anointed by the Spirit, and even the youngest believer has this anointing. You may have been converted only a day or two ago, but the Spirit of God now dwells in you as the anointing, and when you want instruction and power for service, look up to God that He by the Spirit may give you the instruction you need through the Word, and that He may empower you to serve Him.

In the next place we read, "Who hath also sealed us." A seal speaks of ownership. The same Holy Spirit who regenerated us, who baptized us into the Body of Christ, who is our anointing for service and our illumination, dwells within us as the seal that we belong to God. As I look at a group of people I cannot tell a Christian from one who is not converted, but as God looks down He sees every believer in whom the Holy Spirit dwells and says, "That is one of

Mine," and wherever the Holy Spirit is not dwelling in a person, "If any man have not the Spirit of Christ, he is none of His" (Rom. 8:9). The seal is the mark that we belong to Him, "After that ye believed, ye were sealed with that Holy Spirit of promise" (Eph. 1:13). And again we are told in that same epistle to the Ephesians (4:30), "Grieve not the Holy Spirit of God, whereby ye are sealed unto the day of redemption." Notice two things: first, how clearly it brings out the personality of the Holy Spirit. You cannot grieve anything that is not personal. You can grieve those you love the most by bad behavior or coldness or indifference; and so, you may grieve the Holy Spirit of God. The Holy Spirit dwells in you to claim you for Christ, and if you are careless in your life as a believer, allowing worldliness or carnality or anything that is un-Christlike a place in your life, you are grieving the Holy Spirit of God. You might expect it to go on, "Grieve not the Holy Spirit of God, lest He leave you, lest you grieve Him away," but it says, "Grieve not the Holy Spirit of God, whereby ye are *sealed unto the day of redemption.*" This suggests the abiding presence of the Holy Spirit of God. "He which hath begun a good work in you will perform it until the day of Jesus Christ" (Phil. 1:6). When He is come, our Saviour tells us, He shall "abide with you for-

ever" (John 14: 16). The very reason you should
not grieve Him is that He remains within you
whether grieved or ungrieved, but if your behavior is such that you are grieving the Holy
Spirit, you are going to be a very unhappy
Christian. The happy Christian is the one living
in the power of an ungrieved Spirit. It is absolutely impossible to live carelessly and be happy.
The happy Christian is the holy Christian.

The apostle adds, in closing this passage, "And
given the earnest of the Spirit in our hearts."
The Holy Spirit dwelling within us is the earnest
of that full blessing which we are to have at the
coming of our Lord Jesus Christ and our gathering together unto Him, and the more the Holy
Spirit is given His right of way in our lives now,
the more we are permitted to enjoy of that which
shall be ours in all its fulness some day. And so
we see that the filling of the Holy Spirit is connected with the earnest. "Be not drunk with
wine, wherein is excess; but be filled with the
Spirit" (Eph. 5: 18). He lives within us, and
everything that we enjoy of a spiritual nature
we enjoy through the indwelling Holy Spirit.
"But," someone says, "I feel so limited at times;
there is so much I ought to enter into, so much
more God has for me that I do not seem to lay
hold on." Right here comes the admonition, "Be
filled with the Spirit."

Every believer has the Holy Spirit in him as the earnest. Someone says, "But you mean we need more of the Holy Spirit." No, I do not mean that at all. The Holy Spirit is a Person, and He lives in you, and so I do not say you need more of the Holy Spirit, but I do say the Holy Spirit wants to possess more of you. That is the trouble with so many of us, we crowd the Spirit of God off into some one corner of our hearts. A great many of us live our lives almost in airtight compartments. The Holy Spirit can have His place in our religious lives, but what about the home life, the business life, the social life, and even the church life? We often live our lives in these compartments, and when at home we live one way, when at business another, in our social obligations another, and when we go to church another, and then we have our little time of spiritual devotion. There can be no happy, triumphant Christian life until all these partitions are broken down and your life comes entirely under the Spirit of God. Let Him have His way in everything, and there will be a life of victory and blessing. That is what it means to "be filled with the Holy Spirit."

The story is told of a young man who was ashamed of his childhood home and of his mother. He built a beautiful home and had a little place built in the attic for his mother and brought her there to live. But he kept the secret even from his wife as to who she was, until one day she found it out and said to him, "What is this? Your mother hidden away up there in the attic? I never dreamed who was up there."

"Well, you know," he said, "she has never had any education; she isn't accustomed to our way of living, and so I thought it better that she should be hidden away up there."

"No," said the wife, "we will never treat her like that. Your mother is to come down from the attic, and is to have the run of the house and enjoy herself to the fullest degree."

The Holy Spirit of God lives in you, believer. Is He hidden away in the attic of your life or has He the run of the house? Has your life been surrendered to Him? Are you yielded to His control?

You have seen how every operation of the Spirit of God is suggested. But somebody says, "What about the gifts of the Spirit?" He is not speaking here of gifts, but all the gifts are linked with the anointing of the Spirit, and so God has given various gifts to different believers, but it is all through the anointing of the Holy Spirit of God who fits us for any special service which the Lord may have for us.

LED IN CHRIST'S TRIUMPH

✓ ✓ ✓

"Moreover I call God for a record upon my soul, that to spare you I came not as yet unto Corinth. Not for that we have dominion over your faith, but are helpers of your joy: for by faith ye stand. But I determined this with myself, that I would not come again to you in heaviness. For if I make you sorry, who is he then that maketh me glad, but the same which is made sorry by me? And I wrote this same unto you, lest, when I came, I should have sorrow from them of whom I ought to rejoice; having confidence in you all, that my joy is the joy of you all. For out of much affliction and anguish of heart I wrote unto you with many tears; not that ye should be grieved, but that ye might know the love which I have more abundantly unto you. But if any have caused grief, he hath not grieved me, but in part: that I may not overcharge you all. Sufficient to such a man is this punishment, which was inflicted of many. So that contrariwise ye ought rather to forgive him, and comfort him, lest perhaps such a one should be swallowed up with overmuch sorrow. Wherefore I beseech you that ye would confirm your love toward him. For to this end also did I write, that I might know the proof of you, whether ye be obedient in all things. To whom ye forgive anything, I forgive also: for if I forgave anything, to whom I forgave it, for your sakes forgave I it in the person of Christ; lest Satan should get an advantage of us: for we are not ignorant of his devices. Furthermore, when I came to Troas to preach Christ's gospel, and a door was opened unto me of the Lord, I had no rest in my spirit, because I found not Titus my brother: but taking my leave of them, I went from thence into Macedonia. Now thanks

be unto God, which always causeth us to triumph in Christ,
and maketh manifest the savor of His knowledge by us in
every place. For we are unto God a sweet savor of Christ,
in them that are saved, and in them that perish: to the one
we are the savor of death unto death; and to the other the
savor of life unto life. And who is sufficient for these
things? For we are not as many, which corrupt the Word
of God: but as of sincerity, but as of God, in the sight of
God speak we in Christ" (2 Cor. 1: 23-2: 17).

✓ ✓ ✓

THERE are a number of verses in this portion of the Word, any one of which might
furnish the theme for a lengthy address,
but in giving these expositions I cannot pause on
every important verse in the way I should like to
do, but must occupy you rather with the general
trend of the apostle's words, the main thoughts
that are emphasized. I want to confine myself
largely to verses 14, 15, and 16, where the saints
are seen as led in Christ's triumph. But to lead
up to that and to connect with that which we
have had previously, I will go over the intervening verses.

Some of the Corinthians had charged Paul
with lightness, with insincerity, with carelessness,
because he had intimated that he was going to visit
them and then had refrained from doing so.
They said, "Yes, he promises one thing and does
another." Now he explains more fully just why

he did not visit them at an earlier date in accordance with his first intention. "I call God for a record upon my soul, that to spare you I came not as yet unto Corinth. Not for that we have dominion over your faith, but are helpers of your joy: for by faith ye stand." After having made up his mind to visit them he had heard of their very disorderly conduct, they were going to law one with another, petty jealousies had come up among them, there was a sectarian spirit manifested, some were saying, "I am of Paul," others, "I am of Apollos," and still others, "I am of Christ," as though Christ were the Head of a party instead of the Head of the whole Church. And then there were very grievous things of a moral character among them. One had fallen into very marked sin, so much so that the name of God was blasphemed by the world outside because of the wickedness of this professing Christian, and Paul says, as it were, "If I came to you after learning these things I would have to come among you with a rod, simply to scold you, to speak sternly to you, and I could not do that. I loved you so tenderly that I preferred to stay away and write to you and pray for you, and to call upon God to enable you to judge these evil things. Now I am glad to find that you have judged them."

He told them in the previous letter that they

were to put away that wicked man who had
fallen into licentiousness, who was guilty of the
sin of fornication, for otherwise he would corrupt
the whole fellowship. "A little leaven leaveneth
the whole lump" (Gal. 5: 9). "If any man that
is called a brother be a fornicator, or covetous,
or an idolater, or a railer, or a drunkard, or an
extortioner; with such an one no not to eat" (1
Cor. 5: 11). They were to refuse Christian fellowship to such an one, they were to put away
from among them that wicked person. They had
acted upon that, and because they had, he now
feels differently toward them. He did not want
to come until they obeyed his instructions—"But
I determined this with myself, that I would not
come again to you in heaviness. For if I make
you sorry, who is he then that maketh me glad,
but the same which is made sorry by me?" That
is, if when I came to you my time had to be devoted to bringing before you these corrupt things
that have been permitted in your assembly, it
would break my heart. You would be made sad
and I would be sadder, so I stayed away and
prayed and wrote to you. "I wrote this same
unto you, lest, when I came, I should have sorrow
from them of whom I ought to rejoice; having
confidence in you all, that my joy is the joy of
you all." In other words, he said, I had this
confidence that if once these evil things were

really brought to your attention, your Christian conscience would make you see the importance of dealing with them, you would not go on tolerating the wickedness. And that indeed had been true. "For out of much affliction and anguish of heart I wrote unto you with many tears; not that ye should be grieved, but that ye might know the love which I have more abundantly unto you." It was no easy thing for Paul to bring these things to their attention, nor could he do it in a hard, legal way. They were his children in the faith, he loved them tenderly, and it grieved his spirit to find that they had turned aside to evil ways and were bringing dishonor on the name of the Lord Jesus Christ. That should ever be the attitude of a true pastor in the Church of God.

Now he comes to speak particularly of that wicked man who had fallen into the gross sin of immorality and had been put away from Christian fellowship. If every person guilty of immorality in the professed Church could be dealt with and put away today, how much more power there would be in the assemblies of the saints. Of course there is always hidden sin that we cannot deal with, but when it comes to light God's Word demands that it be dealt with and the wicked person put away. We might say, "Well, but if we excommunicate that man, we will drive him from Christian influence and he will get worse and worse." God said, "Deliver such an one unto Satan for the destruction of the flesh, that the spirit may be saved in the day of the Lord Jesus" (1 Cor. 5: 5). Put him outside of the assembly of God, put him back in the world to which he belongs, because he is living according to the world's standards, and leave him there until God brings him to repentance. Then restore him to fellowship,

"If any have caused grief, he hath not grieved me, but in part: that I may not overcharge you all. Sufficient to such a man is this punishment (this discipline), which was inflicted of many." It was not Paul's discipline. Paul had told them what to do, and they did it. The responsibility rests, not on the apostle, but on the Church of God in a given place. And so the Church had inflicted discipline on this man. Now the man is repentant, he proves by his repentance that though he had failed he was really a child of God after all. What will they do with him now? "So that contrariwise ye ought rather to forgive him, and comfort him, lest perhaps such a one should be swallowed up with overmuch sorrow. Wherefore I beseech you that ye would confirm your love toward him." If the devil cannot get the Church of God to overlook outbroken iniquity and to go on as though nothing had happened, he will seek to have them go to the other extreme. If discipline is inflicted upon a person and there is sincere repentance, then the devil will try to harden the hearts of God's people against him. They will say, "We cannot trust that man; he was in our fellowship once, and proved so bad we had to put him out, and we cannot trust him in the future." No, no, the apostle says; you are not to act like that. That is just as wrong as it is to tolerate sin. It is wrong to keep him out when he repents, for what is the Church of God after all but a company of repentant sinners? And what is heaven? It is a home for repentant sinners. No one will ever get into heaven but repentant sinners. I am speaking of adults for, of course, all the little ones are taken home to heaven. There "their angels do always behold the face of My Father which is in heaven" (Matt. 18:10). The Church of God is simply a gathering, not of people who have never failed, but, of repentant sinners, and if a man repents, bring him back into fellowship. Perhaps he feels so defiled, so bad, that he will never ask for restoration. He will say, "I have disgraced the Lord, I am not fit for fellowship." Do not wait for him to ask, go to him and confirm your love toward him. "For to this end also did I write, that I might know the proof of you, whether ye be obedient in all things. Ye were obedient when I said, "Put him away;" now let me see whether you are just as obedient when I say, "Bring him back as a repentant person."

Then he says, "To whom ye forgive anything, I forgive also: for if I forgave anything, to whom I forgave it, for your sakes forgave I it in the person of Christ." He had already forgiven this offender in his own heart. He says, "I have taken that attitude toward this repentant offender. Once I demanded that he be put away, now I forgive him as simply one with you in this act." "Lest Satan should get an advantage of us: for we are not ignorant of his devices." His devices are, first, tolerate sin, and then if you won't do that but you deal with sin in discipline, then never forgive. How often that spirit is manifested among Christians! There is not a great deal of discipline in the Church of God today. A minister said to me one day, "One of our leading members is well known to be supporting a mistress in a hotel down town, and breaking the heart of his wife and children, yet he is a leader in our church, a very wealthy man. If we were to bring him up for discipline it would split the church, and I do not know what we would do without his money." I said, "Better split the church and go on with the godly part. God's Word is clear, 'Put away from among yourselves that wicked person' (1 Cor. 5:13). Let him take his tainted money and go." God does not want the money of a forni-

cator, of an adulterer, of a drunkard, of an extortioner, of a covetous man. He does not need
such money. God has plenty of money to support
His work. Satan says, "Be easy on him; we must
not judge one another." But God's Word says
that we ought to judge those that are within.
When there is outbroken sin we are to deal with
it. The one side is, put him away. But when he
repents and says, "Brethren, I have sinned, but
by the grace of God I have turned from my sin;
will you restore me to your love and confidence?"
what are we to do then? You ought now to forgive. Perhaps he will get so thoroughly under
the power of remorse that he will just break completely and say, "I will never be able to retrieve
myself. The people of God will never have confidence in me again. What difference does it
make what I do?" Show him now that you can
forgive as well as discipline. "Lest Satan should
get an advantage of us."

"Furthermore, when I came to Troas to preach
Christ's gospel, and a door was opened unto me
of the Lord." He had been very near to them;
he was at Troas, which is just across the water,
and he would have liked to go ahead with the
wonderful opportunity for service which came to
him, but he was so restless thinking about their
difficulties that he could not remain. "I had no
rest in my spirit, because I found not Titus my

brother: but taking my leave of them, I went from thence into Macedonia." But no matter what circumstances he is called upon to pass through he says, "Thanks be unto God, which always causeth us to triumph in Christ, and maketh manifest the savor of His knowledge by us in every place." Or, it may be rendered, "Thanks be unto God, which always leadeth us in Christ's triumph." This is a very lovely picture. As Christ's servants we are continually being led in His triumph. What does he mean by that? It is not merely that Christ always makes us victors, but whatever circumstances the people of God may be called upon to pass through we are always led in Christ's triumph. It is a striking figure of speech, a wonderful picture that he puts before us.

When a Roman general had been out into some distant land to put down an uprising, or to win new lands for the Roman empire, to defeat great armies, the senate frequently voted him "a triumph." When he and his army returned to Rome a public holiday was declared, and all the people thronged to the main thoroughfare to see this general enter in triumph. Here is a long line of captives, representatives of the people he has subjugated. They are in chains, and are holding censers in their hands, and sweet, fragrant incense arises. Then comes the general, and behind

him another long line of captives bearing censers.
These in front are to be set at liberty, and the
fragrant incense is the odor of life to them. Those
behind are condemned to die, and are going on
to the arena; they are to be thrown to the
wild beasts or put to death in some other way,
and the fragrant incense that arises from their
censers is a savor of death. The general marches
on in triumph. There are some with a savor of
life, there are others with a savor of death. The
apostle says, as it were, Christ, our great Redeemer, has won a mighty victory over all the
powers of hell. He has led captivity captive and
given gifts unto men. He has annulled him that
had the power of death, and God has voted Him
a triumph; and now Christ is marching triumph-
antly through the universe, and He is leading us
in His triumph, and we who are His captives by
grace are a sweet savor unto life, but even men
who refuse His grace must glorify God in their
judgment, and they are a sweet savor, but unto
death. So he says, "Thanks be unto God, which
always causeth us to triumph in Christ, and
maketh manifest the savor of His knowledge by
us in every place. For we are unto God a sweet
savor of Christ, in them that are saved, and in
them that perish: to the one we are the savor of
death unto death; and to the other the savor of
life unto life. And who is sufficient for these

things?"   As we march on with Christ proclaiming His gospel, that gospel is to God a sweet savor, whether men believe it or refuse to believe it.   But to all who believe it, it is a sweet savor of life; to all who refuse to believe it, it is a savor of death, but its fragrance is just as precious to God whether believed or refused.

"Who is sufficient for these things?"   Let me put it this way: I stand up and try to preach, I attempt to give the gospel of the grace of God knowing my message is to have a double effect, some people are going to believe it, and it will add to their joy for all eternity.   Some people are going to refuse it, and it will make it worse for them than if they had never heard it at all. I may say, "My God, I would rather not preach than make it worse for men in eternity."   But God says, "Go on and preach My Word; it is your business to give it out whether they receive it or reject it.   The responsibility is theirs."   "Who is sufficient for these things?"   "Our sufficiency is of God" (chap. 3: 5).

"For we are not as many, which corrupt the Word of God: but as of sincerity, but as of God, in the sight of God speak we in Christ." That word "corrupt" is a Greek word used for small trading, and suggests the thought of what we call, "grafting."   We are not of those who huckster the Word of God; in other words, we are not of those who are giving out the Word of God for the money we can get out of it, We are not selling the Word of God; we are seeking to minister God's truth for the blessing of His people and the salvation of souls. What a wonderful thing to be led in Christ's triumph! He went down into death, He came up in triumph, having spoiled principalities and powers. He has made a show of them, triumphing over them, and we are linked with Him who says, "I am He that liveth, and was dead; and, behold, I am alive for evermore" (Rev. 1:18).

THE EPISTLE OF CHRIST

✓ ✓ ✓

"Do we begin again to commend ourselves? or need we, as some others, epistles of commendation to you, or letters of commendation from you? Ye are our epistle written in our hearts, known and read of all men: forasmuch as ye are manifestly declared to be the epistle of Christ ministered by us, written not with ink, but with the Spirit of the living God; not in tables of stone, but in fleshy tables of the heart. And such trust have we through Christ to God-ward: not that we are sufficient of ourselves to think anything as of ourselves; but our sufficiency is of God, who also hath made us able ministers of the new testament; not of the letter, but of the spirit: for the letter killeth, but the spirit giveth life" (2 Cor. 3: 1-6).

✓ ✓ ✓

THE first two chapters, which we have already considered, have been largely occupied with the experiences, the trials, and the victories of the apostle Paul and his companions, while they were engaged in the marvelous ministry committed to them of going out into a world of sin to preach the gospel of the grace of God. And now in this third chapter the apostle develops for us in a very striking way the nature of the ministry committed to them, the ministry of the new covenant. He deals in the first place with

65

the epistle of Christ. Notice how he introduces it.

"Do we begin again to commend ourselves? or need we, as some others, epistles of commendation to you, or letters of commendation from you?" What does he mean? Why does he use language like this? As we have noticed on other occasions, one of the greatest trials that the apostle Paul had to meet as he went around in his ministry was the opposition of false brethren, men who professed to be Christians, but who in reality were Jewish legalists who had never apprehended the freeness and the liberty of the gospel, and they were continually dogging his steps. He would scarcely have left a place before they would come in and endeavor to discredit the message by discrediting the messenger. One of their ruses was to call in question his apostleship. For instance, they might put it like this to these Gentile Christians: Paul! Why, he is no true apostle! The apostles were those who were educated by the Lord Jesus Christ when He was here in the flesh, they had their schooling under His own personal instruction. They kept company with Him for three-and-a-half years, and then after He died and ascended to heaven it was they who went forth with authority to proclaim the message of the new covenant. Paul was not one of them, he did not even know Christ when He was here on earth. More than that, he has no commission from the apostolic college at Jerusalem. Challenge him and see. He will tell you he has received no authority from Peter or James or John or any of the rest, authorizing him to go forth on this mission. He simply is a free lance, and you need to be a bit careful of these free lances; you never can tell just what they have up their sleeves. For instance, when Paul visited you did he have a letter of commendation? Did he have a letter from the church at Jerusalem or from one of the other churches, showing that he was in good standing in the place from which he came?

Paul had been in Corinth for a year-and-a-half, and his life had been as an open book. They had seen for themselves the kind of life that he lived, and knew how genuine his profession was. Now he is away from them and is anticipating visiting them again, and some of these Judaizers have said, "If I were you, before giving him the platform I would at least take the precaution of asking him for his letter, and see whether he has a letter of commendation." It is perfectly right and proper, you know, to carry letters. When Apollos, a total stranger, was going from Ephesus to Corinth, Priscilla and Aquila gave him a letter commending, or recommending, him to the confidence of the brethren in Corinth, and as Christians moved from place to place it was right that they should carry a letter, but think of demanding anything like that from the apostle Paul! Why, he says, "Do we then have to accredit ourselves with *you*, you among whom we have labored for a year-and-a-half, you whom we have led to Christ? Is it necessary that now we should have some kind of a letter of commendation? Do we need a letter of commendation to you, or do we need one from you? Is it necessary that we should be commended by you to other people? The fact of the matter is, if it is a letter that is wanted, you yourselves constitute our letter. 'Ye are our epistle written in our hearts, known and read of all men.' If people want to know whether we are genuine or not, they can look at you. Who were you when we came to you? You were poor ungodly heathen, lost in sin, in bondage to iniquity of the very vilest kind, and what are you now? Redeemed men and women who have been brought into the joy and gladness of a new life through the message that we imparted to you. Is not that letter enough? Does that not prove that we are divinely sent? Is not that the Holy Ghost's own *imprimatur*, as it were, put upon our message. 'Forasmuch as ye are manifestly declared to be the epistle of Christ ministered by us.' Through you God is showing what Christ is able to do for sinners who trust Him. We, of course, were the instruments." "Ministered by us, written not with ink, but the Spirit of the living God; not in tables of stone, but in fleshy tables of the heart." God, then, is manifesting Himself to the world through His Church.

In Old Testament times we do not have a message going out to the world as such. God revealed Himself to Israel on Mount Sinai, and gave them His message on tables of stone. Stone, you know, is very hard, very cold, and very unyielding, like the message of the Law itself, but that message was never sent out to the Gentile world. Judaism was not a missionary religion. You never hear of the representatives of Judaism going out into all the world to proclaim the glories of the Old Covenant. Not at all. God had not yet come out to man; He was still dwelling in the thick darkness. The veil was unrent, and God was testing man through one particular nation, the nation of Israel, the very best group He could find. "What things soever the law saith, it saith to them who are under the law: that every mouth may be stopped, and all the world may become guilty before God" (Rom. 3: 19). If the very best people cannot keep the law, there is no use carrying it to the ungodly Gentiles, and so Judaism had no missionary message. Things have changed now. God has come out to men, the veil is rent, the light is shining out, and the message from the risen Christ is, "Go ye into all the world, and preach the gospel to every creature" (Mark 16: 15). And wherever that message is carried, men read its power in the changed lives of those who believe it. That is what the apostle means when he says that we are the epistle of Christ.

I sometimes hear people pray, "O Lord, help us all to be epistles of Christ." You never get it that way in Scripture. It does not say that you are an epistle of Christ and I am an epistle of Christ. It takes the whole Church to make His epistle, but each one of us is one little verse in that epistle. I should hate to have anyone judge Christ simply by me. I hope there is a little of the grace of God seen in my poor life, but take the Church of God as a whole and see what a wonderful letter you have. What a marvelous epistle is God's Church telling the world what the grace of God can do for sinners who trust in Him. And it is such a vital thing, such a tender thing, "written not with ink," but by "the Spirit of the living God; not in tables of stone, but in fleshy tables of the heart." God gives to believers in the gospel a new heart, a new nature, a heart made tender by divine grace, in order that men may go out and manifest the love of Christ to a lost world. The apostle says this gives us confidence, "Such trust have we through Christ to God-ward." If it were not that we could see the change in the life of a man through believing our message we would lose confidence, but when we see His grace working in this miraculous way, then we have trust toward God that we are indeed His chosen servants sent to make known the exceeding riches of His grace.

The epistle to the Philippians (chap. 2: 12-16) gives us a beautiful hint of the way men read the truths of God in the Church of God. "Wherefore, my beloved, as ye have always obeyed, not as in my presence only, but now much more in my absence, work out your own salvation with fear and trembling." I am not to work out my own salvation in my own power but, you see, "It is God which worketh in you both to will and to do of His good pleasure. Do all things without murmurings and disputings: that ye may be blameless and harmless, the sons of God, without rebuke, in the midst of a crooked and perverse nation, among whom ye shine as lights in the world; holding forth the word of life; that I may rejoice in the day of Christ, that I have not run in vain, neither labored in vain." Men, we often say, will not read their Bibles, and we are called upon to live Christ so that as they read us they will see that there is reality in the gospel and the message we preach, because of the change that has come in our lives.

I wish we might test ourselves along that line.

Is my life really witnessing for Christ? Is it
really counting for God? Do the members of my
own family see that God has control of me? Do
they see something of the patience of Christ, the
meekness of Christ, the purity of Christ, something of the love of Christ, the tender compassion
of Christ, in me? Am I manifesting these things?
As I go out in the world, as I mingle with others
in business, in my daily employment, or whatever it may be with which I am occupied, do those
with whom I have to do most intimately see any
difference between me and those who do not make
the profession that I make? Do they say, "Well,
So-and-So may be a Christian; if he is I do not
think much of Christianity?" Or are we so living Christ that others looking upon us say, "Well,
if that is Christianity, I wish I knew something
of it in my own soul"? I have heard people give
testimony like that at times, I have had them
come to me and say, "I have met one of your
people, or, I work with him, and there is something about him that appeals to me; I cannot help
but believe in the reality of the message you
preach because of the effect it has on the people
who believe it." That is what Paul means when
he says that we are the epistle of Christ.

We are Christ's letter. What is a letter for?
It is to express one's mind. And what are some
of the important things in a letter? First, legi-

bility. You want to be able to read it. If you and I constitute the epistle of Christ the letter should be a legible one, one easily read. People ought not to have to puzzle their heads over it and say, "Well, I don't know, I really cannot understand that. It may be Christianity, but it does not seem so to me." And then a letter should contain clear, definite statements. Clearness of meaning characterizes a well-written letter. You do not like to get a letter and go through it all and say, "I can read it, but for the life of me I cannot understand what he means." You and I are called upon to so clearly set forth the grace that is in Christ that people will not have to puzzle over it, but that they will be able to say, "Oh, now I understand; I see what Jesus does for the soul that trusts Him. If that is Christianity, I should like to know the same blessed life my-self." And then, you know, a real letter reveals the personality of the one who writes it. Some-body has said that we have almost lost the art of letter-writing nowadays. Everything is so standardized that our letters do not reveal our personality at all. Take some of the volumes of old-fashioned letters, what a delight it is to take from the book-shelf some of Carlyle's or Brown-ing's letters, and others of the great men of the past. How marvelously they reveal the person-ality, the mentality of the soul, the spirit of those men. The Church is the epistle of Christ, and the Church is expected to reveal to men the personality, the loveliness, the beauty, the preciousness of Jesus. Oh, to have men say, "I did not know Christ until I saw So-and-So, and then I said to myself, 'Jesus must be a wonderful Saviour, for I have seen a little of what He is, revealed in this or that man or woman.'" That is what it means to be an epistle of Christ, to be manifesting Him.

And so the apostle says, it is not that we can do this in ourselves, that we are sufficient of ourselves—"Not that we are sufficient of ourselves to think anything as of ourselves; but our sufficiency is of God." Let us never get away from that. Christianity is a supernatural thing. I am persuaded that one of the greatest mistakes that thousands of people make is to imagine that Christianity is simply a natural thing, a natural life lived on a higher plane than the ordinary life. A man may say, "I think perhaps I have been too selfish, too worldly; I am going to start in and lead a Christian life; I am going to be a Christian, and so am going to join the church, be baptized, take the sacrament, read the Scriptures, and have family prayer." You can do all of those things outwardly, and yet not be a Christian at all. Christianity is not the natural life lived on a higher plane. It is a divine life mani-

fested in the energy of the Holy Spirit. That is
why men need to be born again. That is an old-
fashioned theme, but we cannot emphasize it too
much. The Lord Jesus Christ said to Nicodemus,
a very good man, a very religious man, "Except
a man be born again, he cannot see the kingdom
of God" (John 3: 5). The natural man can manifest only what is in his natural heart; there must
be a second birth. I ask you, in the name of my
Master, Have you ever known that great change
which the Bible calls the new birth? If not, you
have never taken the very first step in the Christian life. You cannot live a Christian life until
you have a Christian life to live. You must receive the life before you can manifest it. "We
are not sufficient of ourselves to think anything
as of ourselves; but our sufficiency is of God."
If you are saying, "I have heard a good deal
about that, but my perplexity is that I do not
know how I may be born again," let me give
you two or three passages from God's Holy Word,
and may His divine Spirit wing them home in
power. John 1: 11: "He came unto His own, and
His own received Him not." How do you receive
Him? You receive Him into your heart, open
your heart to Him, and let Him come in. John
1: 12, 13: "But as many as received Him, to them
gave He power to become the sons of God, even
to them that believe on His name: which were

born, not of blood, nor of the will of the flesh, nor of the will of man, but of God."

Here are three ways by which people do *not* become Christians, and only one way by which they do. "Not of blood." You are not born a Christian because your parents were Christians; the grace of God is not transmitted by natural generation. "That which is born of the flesh is flesh, and that which is born of the Spirit is spirit" (John 3: 6). In the second place, "Nor of the will of man." There is no man so great, so good, that he can make another person into a Christian. We believe in Christian baptism, but he makes a tremendous mistake who supposes that any man can become a Christian through submission to the ordinance of baptism, or that any minister can make another man a Christian by baptism, or by giving the sacrament of the Lord's Supper. In the third place, "Not by his own will." No man can will himself into becoming a Christian. No man can become a Christian by saying, "I have made up my mind, and from now on I am no longer a sinner, I am a Christian." That will no more make him a Christian than a man, who by birth is an American but has become infatuated with the Russian system, can change his nationality by saying, "From now on I am no longer an American, I have decided to be a Russian." You are what you were born, and we were born sinners, and have to be born again in order to become Christians, and so the verse says, "Not of blood, nor of the will of the flesh, nor of the will of man, but of God." There is just one way by which we become Christians, by receiving Christ. Then we are born again. The apostle Peter says, "Being born again, not of corruptible seed, but of incorruptible, by the Word of God, which liveth and abideth for ever...and this is the Word which by the gospel is preached unto you" (1 Pet. 1: 23, 25). When you believe the gospel, when you accept the message that God has given, when you accept the Saviour whom God has sent, then you are born of God, and you become part of this great company designated, "the epistle of Christ." And the same God through whose mighty power we are born again is the One who sends His servants forth to minister His gospel in divine energy.

The apostle concludes this section in verse 6 by saying, "Who also hath made us able ministers (he is not dwelling on his own ability, but the Spirit of God working in and through him has enabled him to minister in power) of the new testament (we do not belong to the old covenant, we are through with that, we are enjoying the spiritual blessings of the new covenant. The word for 'testament' and 'covenant' is exactly the same); not of the letter, but of the spirit." Do

not misunderstand that. When he says "not of
the letter," he does not mean not of the letter of
the Word of God. They tell us that we take the
Bible too literally, and ask us whether we do not
know that "the letter killeth, but the spirit giveth
life." That is what he says here, but by "letter"
he does not mean the literal Word. You cannot
be too literal in reading your Bible. God could
have given it in another way if He meant us to
have it that way, but He wants us to take it as
it is. What is meant here? "The letter" refers
to that which was engraven on the tables of stone,
and therefore "the letter" is the law. But now
you have the new message, the message of the
New Testament, in the energy of the Holy Spirit.
In other words, Paul says, "We are not law
preachers, we do not go to men and say, you must
give up your meanness, you must be obedient to
the law," but we say, "What you cannot do yourselves God is able to do for you by the energizing
power of His Holy Spirit."

If you will open your heart to Christ, He will
give you a new life, and put a new power in you.
He will enable you to live Christ, to be a part of
the epistle of Christ. The letter, the law, could
only kill, could only condemn. It is called in the
verses that follow "the ministration of death,"
but the gospel of God's grace preached in the
power of the Spirit gives life to all who believe.

THE GLORY OF THE NEW COVENANT

✓ ✓ ✓

"But if the ministration of death, written and engraven in stones, was glorious, so that the children of Israel could not stedfastly behold the face of Moses for the glory of his countenance; which glory was to be done away: how shall not the ministration of the Spirit be rather glorious? For if the ministration of condemnation be glory, much more doth the ministration of righteousness exceed in glory. For even that which was made glorious had no glory in this respect, by reason of the glory that excelleth. For if that which is done away was glorious, much more that which remaineth is glorious. Seeing then that we have such hope, we use great plainness of speech. And not as Moses, which put a veil over his face, that the children of Israel could not stedfastly look to the end of that which is abolished: but their minds were blinded: for until this day remaineth the same veil untaken away in the reading of the Old Testament; which veil is done away in Christ. But even unto this day, when Moses is read, the veil is upon their heart. Nevertheless when it shall turn to the Lord, the veil shall be taken away. Now the Lord is that Spirit: and where the Spirit of the Lord is, there is liberty. But we all, with open face beholding as in a glass the glory of the Lord, are changed into the same image from glory to glory, even as by the Spirit of the Lord" (2 Cor. 3: 7-18).

VERSES 7 to 16 of this section constitute a long parenthesis. Let me show you how evident that is. Let us go back and read verses 5 and 6, and then connect with them verse 17, and you will see these two portions are intimately connected and how all the intervening verses come in parenthetically. "Not that we are sufficient of ourselves to think anything as of ourselves; but our sufficiency is of God; who also hath made us able ministers of the new testament; not of the letter, but of the spirit: for the letter killeth, but the spirit giveth life....Now the Lord is that Spirit: and where the Spirit of the Lord is, there is liberty." The apostle leads us through this lengthy parenthesis in order to contrast for us the fading glory of the old covenant with the unchanging, unending glory of the new covenant of grace.

First he says, "If the ministration of death, written and engraven in stones, was glorious, so that the children of Israel could not stedfastly behold the face of Moses for the glory of his countenance; which glory was to be done away: how shall not the ministration of the Spirit be rather glorious?" Notice the two ministries that he contrasts, "the ministration of death" and "the ministration of the Spirit." The ministration of death was the law; the ministration of the Spirit is the gospel of grace. He has already

called the law "the letter," and a very exact translation of the first part of verse 7 would be, "If
the ministration of death, the letter, engraven in
stones, was glorious (and it was), how much
more shall the ministration of grace be glorious?"
The reference, of course, is not to the first giving
of the law but to the second. I wonder whether
we are all familiar with the difference. When
God first gave the law at Sinai He wrote that law
Himself on tables of stone that He had prepared,
and He gave them to Moses amid accompaniments
of thunder and burning fire and a mighty voice
that filled the people's hearts with fear, so that
even Moses himself said, "I exceedingly fear and
quake." He calls that "God's fiery law." It was
absolutely rigid; its principle was, "An eye for
an eye, a tooth for a tooth, burning for burning,
cutting for cutting." It was absolute intrinsic
righteousness. Whatever a man actually deserved
according to that law he was to receive. But
before Moses came down from the mount, the
people had broken that law. The first commandment was, "Thou shalt have no other gods before
Me. Thou shalt not make unto thee any graven
image, or any likeness of any thing that is in
heaven above or that is in the earth beneath, or
that is in the water under the earth. Thou shalt
not bow down thyself to them, nor serve them"
(Exod. 20: 3-5), and before Moses reached the

foot of the mount the people were dancing around
a golden calf.   Moses knew if he had brought
that law into the camp, there could be nothing
but condign judgment.   That holy law would of
necessity have demanded the death of the entire
people, so Moses broke those tables on the side
of the mount, and came down empty-handed, and
then he became the intercessor for the people and
pleaded with God to show mercy.   The Lord said
that He would destroy them but make of him a
great nation.   But Moses said, "Oh, no; if someone has to be destroyed, destroy me, and save the
people," and in that he manifested the spirit of
Christ.   And so he went up into the mount again
for forty days, and this time God gave the law
tempered with mercy, gave it recognizing the fact
that the people themselves would not keep it, but
provided with this second giving of the law a
system of sacrifices whereby the penitent law-
breaker could draw nigh to God with that which
typified the coming into the world of His blessed
Son.   It was still law, but it was law tempered
by grace, and it meant so much to Moses to find
out that the Lord had thoughts of grace in His
heart for the poor people, that when he came
down from the mount his very face was beaming
because of his association with God.   He had
learned to know God in a new way during those
forty days, and when the people saw the light

shining from his face they were amazed, and Moses put a veil over his face until he had done speaking with them, and when he went before the Lord again he took it off. The apostle tells us why he did that.

The thought many of us have had was that Moses put a veil over his face because the glory was so bright that the people could not look upon him, but here we are told by the Holy Spirit that he put a veil over his face because he knew that that glory was fading and passing, and he did not want the people to see the glory disappear. The glory of that covenant could not last because too much depended upon sinful men. And the glory faded and judgment took its place, and so even that second giving of the law proved to be a ministration of death instead of salvation, because of the sinfulness of man's heart. But, says the apostle, if even that ministration came to the people in glory, how much more shall the ministration of the Spirit, the glad wondrous gospel of pure grace, excel in glory! And so we go to-day to a lost world to tell men that God's face is shining with love and compassion upon mankind.

> "Oh, the glory of His grace
>   Shining in the Saviour's face,
>   Telling sinners from above,
>   God is light, and God is love."

"If the ministration of condemnation be glory, much more doth the ministration of righteousness exceed in glory." The law is called, "the ministration of condemnation," because it asked of men an obedience which sinful men were not able to give. The law came demanding righteousness, but the present message of grace is called "the ministration of righteousness," because it comes giving righteousness to men who are unable to produce a righteousness of their own. This is what made it so precious to the apostle Paul. He had spent years of his life trying to produce a righteousness suited for God, but when he caught sight of the risen Christ and heard Him saying, "I am Jesus whom thou persecutest," and knew that blessed Saviour had fulfilled the law for him, that He had died and had been raised again, Paul exclaimed, "That I might be found in Him, not having mine own righteousness, which is of the law, but that which is through the faith of Christ, the righteousness which is of God by faith" (Phil. 3:9). Here is a ministration of glory indeed! "The glorious gospel," it is called elsewhere, "of the blessed God." That word translated "blessed" really means happy. Just think of it—the happy God! What is it that makes God happy? It is because He Himself has found a way whereby His love can go out to guilty sinners, and He can save the very vilest of men and make them fit for His presence. God is a lover of men. Judgment is His strange work, for "He delighteth in mercy" (Micah 7: 18). He hath "no pleasure in the death of the wicked; but that the wicked turn from his way and live" (Ezek. 33: 11). But when He tested men under law, there was nothing but the curse for them, for they could not fulfil its requirements. Now God has met every need of sinful man in the cross of Christ, and He offers an untarnishable righteousness to those who trust His blessed Son. And the heart of God rejoices as His face shines upon sinners.

"For even that which was made glorious had no glory in this respect, by reason of the glory that excelleth." It is like the difference between the moon and the sun. At night as you look upon the moon shining it has wondrous glory, and your heart cannot but be stirred. But have you sometimes seen the moon hanging low upon the horizon after the sun had risen? What a pale, misty, watery-looking thing it was. It was the same moon that shone so brilliantly the night before, but its glory passed away in the light of the glory that excelleth, and so it is that the very highest point to which the Old Testament can bring us, the very highest experiences that Old Testament saints had under the law (and they were glorious in their way, they were precious experiences while they lasted, for there was a glory connected with God's dealing with men under that old covenant), have no glory at all compared with the glory that excelleth. Have you ever noticed that even some of the most devoted saints in Old Testament times were never absolutely sure of their final salvation? Job was in utter bewilderment, David was perplexed, when Hezekiah received word that he was going to die, he turned his face to the wall and wept and sobbed, and was in great distress; but now in this New Testament dispensation of grace, the poorest, feeblest soul that trusts in Jesus may have absolute assurance of his perfect acceptance with God.

An old Scot lay suffering, and his physician had told him it was a matter of only a few hours or a few days at the most. A friend really interested in him came to spend a little time with him and said, "They tell me you will not be with us long. I hope you have got a wee glimpse of the Saviour's blessed face as you are going through the valley of the shadow."

And the dying man said, "Away with the glimpse, man; it's a full view of His blessed face I have had these forty years, and I'll not be satisfied with any of your glimpses now."

That is "the glory that excelleth," the glory that shines in the face of a reconciled God because the sin question has been eternally settled. In view of this, says the apostle, "We use great plainness—or boldness—of speech." I know that to some people the expressions that are used in these New Testament epistles must seem very bold; they cannot comprehend them. Speaking with a Roman Catholic priest a number of years ago about the second coming of the Lord Jesus Christ, I was telling him about the time when "the Lord Himself shall descend from heaven with a shout, with the voice of the archangel, and with the trump of God: and the dead in Christ shall rise first" (1 Thess. 4: 16), and I said, "When that time comes, I am going up with that ransomed throng, I am going to be caught up to be forever with the Lord."

He looked at me a little puzzled, and said kindly, "My dear sir, you must think you are a very great saint to be so sure that you will be taken up at that time."

I said, "No; it is not that I think I am a great saint, I am really one of the least of all saints, and I found out some years ago that I was a great sinner; but I found out that Jesus is a great Saviour, and that He manifests great grace to great sinners by taking all our sins and settling for them on Calvary's cross. And so I trust Him, and trusting Him I know my sins are gone, and therefore I am able to rest in His Word, "If I go ...I will come again, and receive you unto My-

self, that where I am, there ye may be also"
(John 14: 3). "We use great boldness of speech."
I do not know anything but the gospel of the
grace of God that gives this boldness of speech,
this absolute assurance that sins are put away,
and that one is saved for eternity. But this is
the portion of those who have received in their
heart the ministry of reconciliation.

"Seeing then that we have such hope, we use
great plainness of speech. And not as Moses,
which put a vail over his face, that the children of Israel could not stedfastly look to the
end of that which is abolished." Moses covered
his face, as we have seen, that they might not
see the glory fade. That fading glory pictures
this old dispensation that is abolished. There is
nothing of it left for us. There is a new dispensation in which we live which has taken its
place. "But their minds were blinded"—those
who have never moved out of the Old Testament
into the New, they who attach all their hopes to
the Old Testament—"for until this day remaineth
the same veil untaken away in the reading of the
Old Testament; which veil is done away in
Christ."

I wonder whether some of you are my Lord's
own brethren after the flesh, you belong to the
nation of Israel, those whom we call the Jews,
God's earthly people. You are one for whom the

Christian should have the deepest affection. You gave us our Saviour and, under God, you gave us our Bible. God used Jewish hands to write this Bible, and a Jewish mother gave birth to our blessed Lord Jesus Christ, and yet we Christians are enjoying the glory of this new covenant and so many of you, God's earthly people after the flesh, are without this blessing and without this joy. Yet, you still believe your Bible, you still believe the Old Testament, you still believe that those books that comprise the old covenant are really the Word of the living God. You read that Bible and still do not have peace, you have no assurance that your sins are forgiven, you do not know yet for certain that you are right with God, and that if called from this world you would go immediately to Abraham's bosom. Do you know why? Your eyes have not yet been open to see Him of whom Moses and all the prophets spoke. Listen to this word spoken by a Jew, a Jew whose name was Simon Peter. He says, "To Him (that is, to Jesus) give all the prophets witness, that through His name whosoever believeth in Him shall receive remission of sins" (Acts 10: 43). Thousands of Jews have looked through the Old Testament telescope to Christ as the fulfilment of all the types and shadows of the law, the true Messiah of Israel, the promised Redeemer, that Righteousness which God promised to reveal to due time, and, finding Him, the veil has dropped from their hearts and they are rejoicing in the new covenant. This same privilege is yours. "For until this day remaineth the same veil untaken away in the reading of the Old Testament; which veil is done away in Christ." Think of reading the Old Testament with a veil over it, or with the veil over the heart. If you turn to the New Testament and see how wonderfully Christ fulfils all these types and shadows of the law and how truly all the prophecies are fulfilled in Him, the veil will be torn away, and you will be brought out into the full light and liberty of the glory of God. "Even unto this day, when Moses is read, the veil is upon their heart." And that veil will always remain upon their heart until they turn to God in repentance.

"Nevertheless when it shall turn to the Lord, the veil shall be taken away." Observe, it does not simply say, "Nevertheless when they shall turn to the Lord," but it says, "When *it* shall turn to the Lord." To what does the "it" refer? Go back to the preceding noun. "Even unto this day, when Moses is read, the veil is upon their *heart*. Nevertheless when *it* shall turn to the Lord, the veil shall be taken away." That is the end of the parenthetic portion of this section.

Following up what he has already said in verse 6 the apostle concludes the section like this, "Now

the Lord is that Spirit." Our Lord Jesus Christ
is the Spirit of the Old Testament. Turn where
you will in the Old Testament, it has one theme,
and that is Christ. He is the Spirit of the whole
thing, and if you just see the letter and do not
see Him, you have missed the purpose for which
God gave His Book. "The Lord is that Spirit:
and where the Spirit of the Lord is, there is liberty." The Lord Jesus Christ says, "Ye shall
know the truth, and the truth shall make you
free" (John 8: 32). The law puts man in bondage; Christ brings him out into liberty. "Where
the Spirit of the Lord is, there is liberty. But we
all, with open face beholding as in a glass the
glory of the *unveiled face* of the Lord, are
changed (the same word is rendered 'transfigured' in the Gospels) into the same image from
glory to glory, even as by the Spirit of the Lord."
Here is true Christian growth in grace. First,
Christ has to be revealed to the soul, and then as
you go on day after day, as you are occupied with
Christ, you become like Him. You never have to
advertise your holiness, you never have to say,
"See how spiritual I am becoming, how Christlike
I am." This will not be necessary if your heart
is taken up with the Lord Jesus. If occupied with
Him, other people will soon realize that you are
becoming more and more like Him as the days
go by.

You remember Hawthorne's story of "The Great Stone Face." He tells of a lad who lived in the village below the mountain, and there upon the mountain was that image of the great stone face, looking down so solemnly, so seriously, upon the people. There was a legend that some day someone was coming to that village who would look just like the great stone face, and he would do some wonderful things for the village and would be the means of great blessing. The story gripped this lad, and he used to slip away and hour after hour would stand looking at that great stone face and thinking of the story about the one that was coming. Years passed, and that one did not come, and still the young man did what the boy had done, and went to sit and contemplate the majesty, the beauty of that great stone face. By and by youth passed away and middle age came on, and still he could not get rid of that legend; and then old age came, and one day as he walked through the village someone looked at him and exclaimed, "He has come, the one who is like the great stone face!" He became like that which he contemplated. If you want to be Christlike, look at Jesus. If you want to grow in grace, contemplate Jesus. You find Him revealed in the Word, so read your Bible and meditate upon it.

We sing the song,

> "Take time to be holy,
> Speak oft with thy Lord."

Dr. Lewis Sperry Chafer almost always interrupts when this hymn is given out, and says, "Please let me change that first line; let us sing it, 'Take time to behold Him.'" As we behold Him we will become holy, for, "We all, reflecting as in a mirror the glory of the unveiled face of the Lord, are changed, are transfigured, and transformed into the same image from glory to glory, even as by the Spirit of the Lord."

Lecture VII.

THE GOSPEL MINISTRY

✓ ✓ ✓

"Therefore seeing we have this ministry, as we have received mercy, we faint not; but have renounced the hidden things of dishonesty, not walking in craftiness, nor handling the Word of God deceitfully; but by manifestation of the truth commending ourselves to every man's conscience in the sight of God. But if our gospel be hid, it is hid to them that are lost: in whom the god of this world hath blinded the minds of them which believe not, lest the light of the glorious gospel of Christ, who is the image of God, should shine unto them. For we preach not ourselves, but Christ Jesus the Lord; and ourselves your servants for Jesus' sake. For God, who commanded the light to shine out of darkness, hath shined in our hearts, to give the light of the knowledge of the glory of God in the face of Jesus Christ" (2 Cor. 4: 1-6).

✓ ✓ ✓

WE have already noticed that this is preeminently the epistle of Christian ministry, and in the section beginning with these verses the apostle undertakes to open up the nature of that ministry and the responsibilities connected with it.

Notice first, it is something that we have received from God. "Seeing," he says, "that we have this ministry, as we have received mercy, we faint not." I know that the gospel is from God because no man would ever have imagined such a message. I am somewhat familiar with most of the religious systems that have occupied the minds of men. For over forty years this subject has been my study above every other. I am not exaggerating when I say that I have read literally thousands of volumes setting forth the different religious views that have prevailed in this world for the last three or four thousand years of human history, and I want to say that you may put them all together, lump them together in one group, and then put the testimony of the Word of God in another by itself. All human religions teach men that there is something they can do and must do whereby they can placate God and earn their own salvation. The gospel, and the gospel alone, tells men that they are utterly helpless, that they can do nothing to merit divine favor, but that they do not need to do anything, for God Himself has come out in loving-kindness in the Person of His Son to save men by grace alone. This is no human thought; this did not come from the human mind; this is a revelation that came from heaven. We have received this ministry, and having received it we are accountable to God to pass it on to others. It was in His mercy that He made it known to us, and we ourselves have been saved through believing it.

Paul could say that there was a time when he was a Hebrew of the Hebrews, a Pharisee of the Pharisees, when he hoped to work out a righteousness of his own, sufficient to admit him uncondemned into the presence of God. But there came a day when God in infinite grace revealed to Saul of Tarsus his own sinfulness and guilt, when he saw himself, not as a self-righteous Pharisee, but as the chief of sinners, and then in his deep, deep need he turned to Christ alone and found in Him a righteousness for his soul. It meant something to him when he said, "We have received this ministry." He was referring to a very definite personal experience that he had gone through. I am wondering whether you know something of that; I wonder whether you have ever been brought by the Spirit of God to see your own innate sinfulness, your guilt, your lost condition, and not only your lost condition but your utter helplessness. I wonder whether God has ever revealed to you His own blessed Son in whom "dwelleth all the fulness of the Godhead bodily" (Col. 2:9), who came in grace from the heights of glory to the cross of shame and there gave Himself a ransom for all. "But He was wounded for our transgressions, He was bruised for our iniquities: the chastisement of our peace

was upon Him; and with His stripes we are
healed" (Isa. 53:5). Receiving such mercy, what
a responsibility now rests upon you to make it
known to others. The apostle is speaking not
merely of what we may call the official ministry of
the Church, of a man who proclaims the gospel
from the public platform, when he says, "As we
have received mercy," but every Christian is the
object of mercy, and therefore should boldly go
forth to proclaim the gospel of the grace of God
to others. We are not afraid now, we do not lose
heart, as we go to men telling of great grace for
great sinners.

On the other hand, the apostle Paul emphasizes
the importance of living the gospel. He says,
"We have renounced the hidden things of dishonesty." It is not merely an intellectual thing
with us. It is not simply that we come to the
conclusion, after the process of logical investigation, that Jesus Christ is the divine, eternal Son
of God, and confess that as a creedal statement,
but we have turned to Him in heart, and turning
to Him we have been delivered from our sins, and
we have renounced those things in which once
we lived, in which once we gloried, the activities
of the flesh fulfilling the desires of the flesh and
of the mind. The cross of Christ has brought
these things to an end. In other words, the pro-
claimer of the gospel must himself be a holy man,

he must live the truth that he preaches to other people. "We have renounced the hidden things of shame (*margin*), not walking in craftiness," not walking in guile, nor hypocrisy. There is nothing that is unreal, nothing that cannot bear the light in our behavior, but there is only that which can have the approval of the Lord Jesus Christ.

"Nor handling the Word of God deceitfully." Somebody has translated that, "Nor huckstering the Word of God." We go to men and proclaim the gospel and tell them we are doing it for love of their souls. What a sinful thing if, when I profess to proclaim the gospel for love of the souls of men I should, after all, simply be preaching it for love of the money which might come to me, because Christ has said that they that preach the gospel should live of the gospel. If I am going to devote all of my time to the preaching of the gospel, it is necessary that I be supported in some way, but if I make that the object, if I go out to preach as though simply performing something for which I am looking for temporal support, then I am a hypocrite and a sham, I am dealing with God's truth as though it were butter and eggs and groceries. The apostle says we are not to do that. Paul might have been a wealthy man if he had pursued the path for which he was trained in early life. He might have been one of

the most widely-recognized professors in Judea.
He chose to become poverty-stricken in order to
go out and preach Christ, and he was even ready
to work with his hands making tents, when necessary to support himself and his companions. The
preaching of the gospel was a commission given
to him by the risen, glorified Lord, and he could
say, "Woe is me if I preach not the gospel."

"Nor handling the Word of God deceitfully;
but by manifestation of the truth commending
ourselves to every man's conscience in the sight
of God." I know it is possible to preach the gospel and to say things that are perfectly true, and
yet the life that is back of the speaking be contrary to the message delivered. In a case like
that there is no real power. The power of the
Word is found when a man is walking with God
in communion with the Holy Spirit. I have
prayed thousands of times, and I dare to pray
again, knowing that God may take me at my word
if I fail, "O God, keep me from ever being able
to preach the gospel without a clear conscience
and the power of the Holy Ghost." To attempt
to do it is but to mock God, and to mock men for
whom Christ died. "By manifestation of the
truth commending ourselves to every man's conscience in the sight of God."

The remarkable thing is that one can preach
this gospel and yet not have men understand it;

it does not seem to appeal to them. In the third chapter we read that when Moses is read there are certain ones who are blinded, and they cannot see that he speaks of Christ. But the same thing is true in the New Testament. You can preach it, men may sit down over the New Testament and read it carefully, and still it seems hazy, it seems that there is a veil over it. How do you account for that? Is the gospel then no clearer than the message of the Old Testament? How do you account for the apparent veil that hangs over the hearts of men as they read or hear the gospel? He explains it for us by saying, "If our gospel be hid (or veiled), it is veiled to them that are lost: in whom the god of this world hath blinded the minds of them which believe not." The god of this world, or the god of this age, is Satan. That is a wonderful expression to use of him. The Lord Jesus called him the "prince of this world," and now the apostle Paul by the Holy Spirit goes farther and calls him the "god of this age." The devil is the only god that Christless men know; they are led by the devil captive to his will. There are men who even deny his existence, but the very fact that they refuse the gospel message shows that they are under his power. "If our gospel be veiled, it is veiled to them that are lost." Do you say, "I do not understand; I have heard this all my life, but it means nothing to me; I have heard those words over and over and over again, but they do not register with me, they do not mean anything to me"? Is that true of you? Then let me tell you seriously, tenderly, earnestly, the reason that you are lost, lost deliberately, wilfully, is because of your own sin. That is why you cannot see nor apprehend the beauty, the preciousness of the gospel. "If our gospel be veiled, it is veiled to them that are lost; in whom the god of this world hath blinded the minds of them which believe not, lest the light of the glorious gospel of Christ, who is the image of God, should shine unto them." It is Satan that holds you in his control. The reason you cannot believe is that you do not want to believe. If you would believe, it would mean the judging of those things in your life that are contrary to the Word of God. If any man says, "There are things in the Bible that I cannot believe," I can tell him why. It is because there are things in his life that the Bible condemns, of which he does not wish to repent. There are sins that mean more to him than Christ. He would rather indulge in them than be delivered from them. The moment a man comes to the place where he desires God's will above all else, and says, "I am ready to renounce my sin, to be freed from it," that man will not have any trouble believing the gospel. Judge yourself in the presence of God, and you will be able to believe Him. Face your sins before God, and there will be no difficulty about believing.

Someone said to Sir Isaac Newton, "Sir Isaac, I do not understand; you seem to be able to believe the Bible like a little child. I have tried, but I cannot. So many of its statements mean nothing to me. I cannot believe; I cannot understand."

Sir Isaac Newton replied, "Sometimes I come into my study and in my absent-mindedness I attempt to light my candle when the extinguisher is over it, and I fumble about trying to light it and cannot; but when I remove the extinguisher then I am able to light the candle. I am afraid the extinguisher in your case is the love of your sins; it is deliberate unbelief that is in you. Turn to God in repentance; be prepared to let the Spirit of God reveal His truth to you, and it will be His joy to show the glory of the grace of God shining in the face of Jesus Christ."

Those who believe not do not desire this knowledge, "lest the light of the glorious gospel of Christ, who is the image of God, should shine unto them." It says in our Authorized Version, "The glorious gospel." That is precious, but it does not really give us the whole truth. It is not only that the gospel is in itself glorious, but the gospel that we preach is not a gospel of earth but it is the gospel of the glory of Christ. Christ is up there in glory at God's right hand, and from the risen, glorified Christ comes this message of reconciliation to sinful men. That is why the apostle speaks of it in the way he does. Christ is the image of God, the manifestation of God. How Satan wants to keep men from coming into this place, and how God is yearning to have men know Him as revealed in His Son.

The gospel is not just a philosophy. What are men's philosophies after all? Philosophy is the acting of mind upon mind, trying to explain things in a logical, reasonable, human way, and the stronger the mind of the speaker the more it impresses other people, and brings them to think as he thinks. Men depend upon logic, rhetoric, and eloquence in order to impress their fellows. But it was not so with the apostle Paul. He was afraid that mere human reason might overrule the power of the gospel, and so said, "Not with wisdom of words" (1 Cor. 1: 17). Men like to hear lovely figures of speech expressed in beautiful language, but the business of the gospel preacher is not simply to reach the mind of man but to reach his conscience and his will, and when man's conscience is exercised and his will is turned toward God, then his soul is saved through faith in Christ. But this is not the result of human effort, this is the work of the Holy Spirit, and that is why the servant of Christ needs to put his dependence entirely upon the Spirit of God.

Notice how the apostle closes this section. "For we preach not ourselves, but Christ Jesus the Lord; and ourselves your servants for Jesus' sake." He could not say in plainer words, "We are not trying to attract attention to ourselves, we do not want the result of our ministry to be that men will go about and say, 'What a wonderful preacher Paul is! What an eloquent man is Apollos! What a marvelous exhorter is Simon Peter! How wonderful these men are!' " I have often felt ashamed at the foolish things well-meaning men have said in introducing servants of Christ to an audience. They make so much of the man, they have so much to say about his ability and his accomplishments, when it is only through the power of the Holy Ghost that he can do anything at all. We should never forget that it is the Saviour who counts, and the Word that God uses in the power of the Holy Ghost. So Paul says, "We preach not ourselves," we do not want to attract attention to ourselves. Like John the Baptist we say, "He must increase, but I must decrease" (John 3: 30). "We preach Christ Jesus the Lord," and it is only as He is exalted that men and women are blessed. It is only as He is exalted that sinners are saved. But what of the preacher? "Ourselves your servants for Jesus' sake." That is all; just "your servants for Jesus' sake."

"For God, who commanded the light to shine out of darkness, hath shined in our hearts, to give the light of the knowledge of the glory of God in the face of Jesus Christ." Away back there in the beginning God looked upon a world of chaos wrapped in night, and the Spirit of God moved upon the face of the deep, and God said, "Let there be light, and there was light," and He who "commanded the light to shine out of darkness hath shined in our hearts, to give the light of the knowledge of the glory of God in the face of Jesus Christ." This is our ministry, to bring all men to see the beauty of Christ, to see that, "In Him dwelleth all the fulness of the Godhead bodily" (Col. 2: 9), that He is indeed the light of life.

> "I heard the voice of Jesus say,
> 'I am this dark world's Light;
> Look unto Me, thy morn shall rise,
> And all thy days be bright.'
> I looked to Jesus, and I found
> In Him my Star, my Sun;
> And in that light of life I'll walk,
> Till traveling days are done."

Have you seen "the glory of God in the face of Jesus"?

LECTURE VIII.

PRESENT TRIAL AND FUTURE GLORY

✓ ✓ ✓

"For God, who commanded the light to shine out of darkness, hath shined in our hearts, to give the light of the knowledge of the glory of God in the face of Jesus Christ. But we have this treasure in earthen vessels, that the excellency of the power may be of God, and not of us. We are troubled on every side, yet not distressed; we are perplexed, but not in despair; persecuted, but not forsaken; cast down, but not destroyed; always bearing about in the body the dying of the Lord Jesus, that the life also of Jesus might be made manifest in our body. For we which live are alway delivered unto death for Jesus' sake, that the life also of Jesus might be made manifest in our mortal flesh. So then death worketh in us, but life in you. We having the same spirit of faith, according as it is written, I believed, and therefore have I spoken; we also believe, and therefore speak; knowing that He which raised up the Lord Jesus shall raise up us also by Jesus, and shall present us with you. For all things are for your sakes, that the abundant grace might through the thanksgiving of many redound to the glory of God. For which cause we faint not; but though our outward man perish, yet the inward man is renewed day by day. For our light affliction, which is but for a moment, worketh for us a far more exceeding and eternal weight of glory; while we look not at the things which are seen, but at the things which are not seen: for the things which are seen are temporal; but the things which are not seen are eternal" (2 Cor. 4: 6-18).

THE verse with which we began our reading links very clearly with the first chapter of the book of Genesis. You remember we read, "In the beginning God created the heaven and the earth." Some people imagine that we who are generally dubbed "fundamentalists" believe that that took place at about 10 o'clock in the morning in the year 4004 B.C. We do not believe anything of the kind. I have never yet met a fundamentalist who had any such crude conception of the time of creation. What we do believe is that whenever creation took place, no matter how many millions or billions of years back, it was God who brought everything into existence— "In the beginning God created the heaven and the earth." We do not know the exact condition of the earth at that time, except that we are told in Isaiah 45: 18 that "He created it not 'in vain' (or void), He formed it to be inhabited." The earth, as God originally created it, was absolutely perfect, but the second verse of Genesis tells us that "the earth became without form, and void." Something happened to that first creation; there was a fall, some great catastrophe happened, and so we have the condition depicted in that second verse. Therefore God began to work again in order to fit up this earth that it might be the stage upon which would be played the wondrous drama of redemption.

We are told that, "The Spirit of God brooded over the face of the deep. And God said, Let there be light: and there was light." Notice two things: the Spirit of God brooded—God spake. "The entrance of Thy words giveth light" (Ps. 119: 130). We think of man as in very much the same condition as at that fall. "God hath made man upright" (Eccl. 7:29), but he fell and lost the robe of glory. We say, "Necessity is the mother of invention," and the first invention was that of the fig-leaf apron. Realizing his nakedness Adam made for himself an apron of fig-leaves. Through sin man fell into this chaotic condition, but God was going to work in order to lift him out of it. Man is in darkness, he is lost and wretched, and in redeeming him two great things are involved: first, the brooding of the Holy Spirit over the soul of man, for no man has ever been saved apart from the work of the Holy Spirit. The second thing is the message of the gospel. "God said, Let there be light: and there was light." And here we read, "God, who commanded the light to shine out of darkness, hath shined in our hearts, to give the light of the knowledge of the glory of God in the face of Jesus Christ." And so we to whom that light has come, we who have believed the gospel message, have been brought out of nature's darkness into this marvelous light of God, through the gospel.

The apostle now shows that we are intrusted with this message, to carry it to poor, lost men and women. We ourselves are just feeble, sinful creatures, not perfect by any means, but having a perfect Saviour to proclaim and perfect salvation to preach. And so he says, "We have this treasure in earthen vessels (he means our bodies), that the excellency of the power may be of God, and not of us." I think you can see that the reference here is to the battle in the days of Gideon when his little army of three hundred surrounded the great camp of the Midianites. To every one of those soldiers had been intrusted an earthen vessel, and in that vessel was a light, a lamp of some kind. Gideon told the soldiers to surround the camp and to do whatever he did, and so at a given time he cried, "The sword of Jehovah and of Gideon," and he broke the earthen vessel and the light shone out. The moment he did that, all the others did the same thing, and the Midianites sprang to their feet and thought there must be a tremendous army surrounding them. They felt there was no hope, and in their distress in the darkness they began to kill each other, and so Gideon's army was victorious. It was a great victory won in a peculiar way. That is what every Christian is, an earthen vessel with a light in it. To you and to me there has been committed the glorious light of the gospel. We were once in darkness but are now in the light of the Lord. In order for a light to shine out of a vessel it has to be broken. Do you know why some people who know the gospel intellectually never win a soul to Christ? It is because the earthen vessel has never been broken, they have never been humbled and cast down in the presence of God. One may know all about the way of life and yet never communicate light to others, because that one has never been broken in the presence of God. "We have this treasure in earthen vessels, that the excellency of the power may be of God, and not of us." The vessel has nothing to boast of; it is the light that accomplishes everything.

The apostle is thinking particularly of himself and his fellow-workmen when he says, "We are troubled on every side, yet not distressed." We to whom has been committed the glorious ministry of the gospel, realize that we are to expect trouble. "We are perplexed," often we hardly know which way to turn. But we are not in despair because we are assured that our blessed Master understands, and we are waiting word from Him. "Persecuted, but not forsaken."

"Let the world despise and leave me,
    They have left my Saviour too,
Human hearts and looks deceive me,
    Thou art not like them untrue."

"In the world," says the Lord Jesus, "ye shall have tribulation; but be of good cheer, I have overcome the world" (John 16: 33). Our risen, glorified, triumphant Saviour backs up every one of His persecuted, suffering people. "Always bearing about in the body the dying of the Lord Jesus." That simply means that we who are Christians are daily delivered over to death; that is, the power of the gospel of Jesus Christ is being made manifest in our daily lives. The Lord Jesus says, "If any man will come after Me, let him deny himself, and take up his cross, and follow Me" (Matt. 16: 24). If you had been living in the days when the Lord uttered those words, and you had seen a company of soldiers coming down the road, and a man in the midst bearing a cross on his shoulders, you would have said, "That man is going out to death." Very well, "That is the place I want you to take for Me," our Lord is saying. "He that loseth his life for My sake shall find it" (Matt. 10: 39). Take that place for Me, take the cross and follow Me. No matter what comes you are simply to be yielded, even to death, in order to glorify Me. That is what we glory in. "Always bearing about in the body the dying of the Lord Jesus." Elsewhere the apostle says, "I die daily" (1 Cor. 15: 31). I wonder if any servant of Christ has ever suffered and endured more than the apostle Paul. But he gloried in it all because as he suffered for Jesus' sake, the life of Jesus was being made manifest in his mortal body. Men could look at him and say, That is the way Christ would have us live. And so you and I are called upon to manifest the life of the Lord Jesus Christ.

"We which live are alway delivered unto death for Jesus' sake, that the life also of Jesus might be made manifest in our mortal flesh. So then death worketh in us, but life in you." He is speaking, you see, as a servant of Christ who had been broken in order that the light might shine, in order to illuminate the darkened hearts of those Corinthians. We have been given up to tribulation, trial, and persecution that the light may shine through us to a lost world. That was so with the Lord Jesus Christ. He said, "Except a corn of wheat fall into the ground and die, it abideth alone: but if it die, it bringeth forth much fruit" (John 12:24), and the same principle applies in regard to His servants. If you want to be of use to the Lord Jesus Christ, you must be prepared to take the place of death.

It was Arthur T. Pierson, I believe, who when visiting George Mueller asked him, "Mr. Mueller, would you be willing to tell me the secret of your great work and the wonderful things that God has done through you?"

Mr. Mueller looked up for a moment, and then

bowed his head lower and lower until it was down between his knees, and he was silent a moment or two, and then said, "Many years ago there came a day in my life when George Mueller died. As a young man I had a great many ambitions, but there came a day when I died to all these things, and I said, 'Henceforth, Lord Jesus, not my will but Thine,' and from that day God began to work in and through me."

General Booth expressed it in a different way. J. Wilbur Chapman said to him, "Will you tell me the secret of the great work that you have accomplished?"

He said, in his straightforward way, as he looked right into the face of Doctor Chapman with that eagle eye of his, "Dr. Chapman, when I was a lad of seventeen, I determined that God should have all there was of William Booth."

That is it! When I come to the place where I am through with my own ambitions, when I can say, "None of self, but all of Thee," I understand what Paul means when he talks about "Bearing about in the body the dying of the Lord Jesus."

"So then death worketh in us, but life in you. We having the same spirit of faith, according as it is written, I believed, and therefore have I spoken; we also believe, and therefore speak." No man can live the life that Paul speaks of unless he has by faith seen the Lord Jesus Christ, the risen One up yonder. Who would want to identify himself with a dead Christ? But Christ has been raised again, and believing we speak of the mighty triumph of faith.

"Knowing that He which raised up the Lord Jesus shall raise up us also by Jesus, and shall present us with you. For all things are for your sakes, that the abundant grace might through the thanksgiving of many redound to the glory of God. For which cause we faint not; but though our outward man perish, yet the inward man is renewed day by day. For our light affliction, which is but for a moment, worketh for us a far more exceeding and eternal weight of glory." Notice the many striking contrasts in these verses. First observe the contrast between perishing and being renewed. "For which cause we faint not; but though our outward man perish, yet the inward man is renewed day by day." The outward man perisheth. How well we know that! What is the outward man? It is the physical man, the body, and many of us realize that the outward man is perishing. There is not the elasticity in the step that there used to be, there is not the physical vigor that there once was. We tire a great deal more easily than we did some years ago. We do not remember things as well as we once did. And some of us have noticed a very strange thing about memory. We can recall very vividly things that happened away back in our early years; we remember the little incidents of childhood days, we remember the people who were kind to us in those days, and some of us have never gotten over the remembrance of those who were very unkind to us. We remember very vividly the experiences of our early school-days and many of our early spiritual experiences, the time when God spoke to our young hearts, the exercises we went through, and then the moment of decision when we accepted Christ. These things we remember very well, but have a great deal of difficulty remembering what happened yesterday. We even go home from a meeting and some one says, "Was it a good sermon?"

And we say, "I think it was; yes, reasonably so."

"Well, what was the text?"

"Well, I declare, I forget," and we cannot call it back. Memory plays all kinds of queer tricks on us. Yes, the outward man is perishing, but "the inward man is renewed day by day."

The inward man is the spirit, the soul, the real man, regenerated by the power of the Holy Ghost. The body gets weaker and weaker, but the inward man gets stronger and stronger. The nearer we get to heaven, the more real the precious things of the Lord become to us. I think Bunyan's picture is a very lovely one. He

saw the aged saints lying on the shores of the
river of life in the land of Beulah, and they could
get glimpses every now and then of the glory of
the celestial city.   At times they could actually
see the shining ones from the other side, and at
others they thought they could even hear the
voices of the saints and their songs of praise.
I think the aged know much of that. God's
saints who have lived for Him through the years,
and now have gotten very close to the end of this
life, already seem to get the sounds and sights
from the celestial city yonder to which they are
going; and be assured that these things will become more and more real to you the closer
you get to the end.   "At eventide, it shall be
light."

"Our light affliction, which is but for a moment,
worketh for us a far more exceeding and eternal
weight of glory." Here again we see a vivid contrast; first, the contrast between affliction and
glory. You have known much of affliction as you
have gone along the way. You have not lived
your life without knowing a great many trials
and afflictions; you have not failed to know suffering and bereavement and disappointment.
There are times when the tears will flow. But
now God puts in contrast to the affliction which
you have known down here the glory that is coming by-and-by, and if the affliction has oppressed

your heart, how the glory will overwhelm you when you are at Home with Christ.

He speaks of the affliction as "light affliction," but of the glory as a "weight" of glory. You have sometimes felt as though your affliction was very heavy, but it has no real weight at all in comparison with the glory that is coming. Therefore, if the affliction seems to have been very heavy when God calls it light, you can get some idea of the glory that awaits us. He says, "Our light affliction, which is but for a moment." It does not seem as though it has been just "for a moment." I was talking to a dear saint who for over twenty years had been sitting in a wheelchair, and I said, "It is good to know that the Lord is coming, and then all this trouble will be over."

"Oh, yes," she said; "but it is so long, it has lasted so long. I wonder when it ever will come to an end."

It seemed a long time, yet he says it is but for a moment. Suppose that one had spent his whole lifetime in this world in affliction and had lived to be seventy, eighty, or ninety years of age; after all, what is that compared with eternity? "We spend our years as a tale that is told" (Ps. 90: 9). Our years pass as "a watch in the night" (Ps. 90: 4). "Our light affliction is but for a moment."

But notice what awaits us on the other side. "Our light affliction, which is but for a moment, worketh for us a far more exceeding and eternal weight of glory." How strongly he puts that! It gives some conception of what is coming, what it will be by-and-by, when earth's trials are past and we are at last in the glory with the Lord Jesus.

In the meantime, "We look not at the things which are seen, but at the things which are not seen: for the things which are seen are temporal; but the things which are not seen are eternal." We are not to be occupied with present things that we see, but we should seek to be occupied with the things that are not seen, for they are, after all, the real things, the eternal things. The things that no human eye has seen are the things that are lasting. When everything that the eye looks upon will have vanished, we shall have Christ, we shall have Heaven, we shall have the Holy Spirit, we shall have the love of the Father, we shall have communion with the people of God for all eternity, when earth's vain shadows have passed away.

THE
STATE OF THE BELIEVER BETWEEN
DEATH AND RESURRECTION

✓ ✓ ✓

"For we know that if our earthly house of this tabernacle were dissolved, we have a building of God, an house
not made with hands, eternal in the heavens. For in this
we groan, earnestly desiring to be clothed upon with our
house which is from heaven: if so be that being clothed we
shall not be found naked. For we that are in this tabernacle do groan, being burdened: not for that we would be
unclothed, but clothed upon, that mortality might be swallowed up of life. Now He that hath wrought us for the
selfsame thing is God, who also hath given unto us the
earnest of the Spirit. Therefore we are always confident,
knowing that, whilst we are at home in the body, we are
absent from the Lord: (for we walk by faith, not by sight:)
we are confident, I say, and willing rather to be absent
from the body, and to be present with the Lord" (2 Cor.
5: 1-8).

✓ ✓ ✓

IN any discussion of the state of the believer
between death and resurrection it is absolutely necessary, if we are to be at all intelligent as to it, to realize something of the truth of
these verses. The first thing that we need to have
clear in our minds is that there is an outward man
and in inward man. The two are not to be con-

119

founded.   There are materialists of different
stripes who insist that the only man there is is
the man that we can see from day to day, and
that when death comes the entire man is laid
away in the tomb, as some think, to remain in
an unconscious sleep until the day of resurrection.
But when we turn to the Word of God we do
not find any such confusion of the outward with
the inward man.   The outward man is the physical man, the man that we see with the natural
eye; the inward man is the man who dwells within this body, and that man we cannot see.   I
look over a great audience and I can see thousands of human forms, but I cannot see the inward man in any instance; I see only the outward.   As you look up to the platform and see
those of us standing or seated here, you are looking only at the tabernacles, the tabernacles of
flesh in which we live.

You cannot really see us, for spirit is invisible
to the natural eye.   "The things which are seen
are temporal; but the things which are not seen
are eternal."   God is Spirit, and yet God is real.
He "maketh His angels spirits" (Ps. 104: 4), and
yet angels are real.   God is a Person; angels are
personalities, and you and I are spirit personalities living for a little while in mortal bodies.
But now see what we are told in the opening
verses of this fifth chapter.

"We know that if our earthly house of this tabernacle were dissolved (that is, if this tenement of clay, this physical body passes away, even though it goes back to its native element, as is so often the case after being put away in the grave, if that should take place), we have a building of God, an house not made with hands, eternal in the heavens." Notice the distinction in every instance between ourselves and the houses in which we now live. Our earthly house is dissolving. Today I am looking into the faces of many who are growing old. It is a wonderful thing to grow old in Christ. Personally, I rejoice in every year that goes by. People say sometimes, "I don't like getting old." To be perfectly frank, I do, because I feel that every passing year is bringing me nearer the glory land, every passing year is bringing me nearer the time when I shall see the face of Him who loved me and gave Himself for me. Then too every passing year means just so much less conflict with the world, the flesh, and the devil, and you know the Christian life is a conflict. How many temptations we have had to face! At times we have yielded, and other times through grace we have been enabled to overcome, but what a wonderful thing it will be when there is no more conflict, and no possibility of failure.

The old house is breakng down; with some of

us the roof is thatched now with white hair, and we are reminded that day by day we shall soon move out unless Christ Himself returns. But we are not disheartened, we are not discouraged, for "though our outward man perish, yet the inward man is renewed day by day." My hope is brighter now than it ever was; my joy in Christ is greater than it has ever been; the world means less to me today than it has ever meant, and the applause of men means less. But the approval of the Lord means more than it has ever meant. I do not feel that I am getting old, it is just the body, the outward man that is perishing, just the old house that is breaking down. I am just as certain that I "have a building of God, an house not made with hands, eternal in the heavens," awaiting me, as I am that I am living in this tenement of clay, and that body will be like the glorified body of the Lord Jesus Christ. I do not enter that new body the moment I die. Some have thought that this scripture teaches that when we leave this world we find awaiting us in heaven a body that serves us between death and resurrection, and then in resurrection we shall have a glorified body that takes the place of this intermediate body. But the verse itself contradicts that thought. It says this house not made with hands abides *"eternal* in the heavens." Between death and resurrection we pass out of the body and our pure spirits enter into the presence of the Lord.

"In this we groan." That is a scripture I do not have to expound to you. You live it out; you know what it is to groan. There are many things to make us do so. Some of us used to groan in the bondage of sin, but though delivered from that, we are still groaning as we wait for a resurrection body. There are so many aches and pains and sorrows and sufferings. "In this we groan, earnestly desiring to be clothed upon with our house which is from heaven." That is, we are yearning for the time when we shall have our new body, we are looking forward to resurrection or change at the coming of our Lord Jesus Christ and our gathering together unto Him.

But mark, even resurrection will not be a blessing if we are not robed in divine righteousness. And so the apostle puts in a word here lest people take it for granted that resurrection means salvation, for there shall be a "resurrection both of the just and unjust" (Acts 25: 15), "They that have done good, unto the resurrection of life; and they that have done evil, unto the resurrection of damnation" (John 5: 29). And so he speaks of resurrection as a "clothing upon." "If so be that being clothed we shall not be found naked." Writing to the church at Laodicea, where a great many who professed the name of the Lord were not really born again, the Saviour says, "Thou sayest, I am rich, and increased with goods, and have need of nothing; and knowest not that thou art wretched, and miserable, and poor, and blind, and naked" (Rev. 3:17). What a solemn thing it would be to stand before God as one risen from the dead and yet spiritually naked in His presence. You say, "Where can we find clothing suitable for the eyes of God?" It is that which He Himself provides. Isaiah says, "He has clothed me with the garments of salvation, He hath covered me with the robe of righteousness" (Isa. 61:10). And so in that day when we are raised from the dead or are changed by power divine, if we live to greet Him when He returns, we who have trusted Christ shall not be found naked, we shall be clothed in the righteousness of God.

"We that are in this tabernacle do groan, being burdened: not for that we would be unclothed," we are not earnestly desiring to die, for that would not be a natural thing for any Christian. The Christian should not earnestly desire to die, and yet should be prepared for it, but he should also be prepared to live for the glory of the Lord Jesus Christ. Paul says, "For me to live is Christ, and to die is gain" (Phil. 1:21). And then he says that he would rather live to be a

help and blessing to other people. And so we hope
"not for that we would be unclothed," but we do
long to be "clothed upon." That is, we would like
to live to the second coming of our Lord Jesus
to get our resurrection body in that wonderful
hour of His triumph, "that mortality might be
swallowed up of life." And whether we live or
die this is the final goal.

"Now He that hath wrought us for the selfsame thing is God, who also hath given unto us
the earnest of the Spirit." It is a settled thing
with God that some day we are going to have
glorified bodies, and as proof of this He has already given us His blessed Holy Spirit to dwell
within us, and He is the earnest of the joy that
shall be ours by-and-by when we gather in His
presence in the Father's house. Because of this
assurance, "We are always confident, knowing
that, whilst we are at home in the body, we are
absent from the Lord." We have no doubt as we
think of any eventuality, whether living until
Christ comes or dying. Notice that expression,
"At home in the body." I (the real I) am living
in this body; the body is my house, my temporary
house. I am at home in the body but I am absent
from the Lord. He is up there in the glory. True,
He has given me His Holy Spirit, as we have
just seen, and by Him He dwells within me, but
actually I am absent from the Lord. "For we

walk by faith, not by sight." We take His word for it—faith is taking God at His word. We are living in the body, and are absent from the Lord, but, "We are confident, I say, and willing rather to be absent from the body, and to be present with the Lord." It will be even more blessed for us to be absent from the body and to be present with the Lord. Here then in one verse we have summed up for us the believer's state between death and resurrection. When death comes for the Christian, in that moment the believer is absent from the body and at home with Christ.

Observe, he does not go to sleep in the body. The "soul-sleepers" insist that in the hour of death the believer becomes absolutely unconscious and knows nothing until the resurrection. You may ask, But has he not scripture for that? Does not the Bible speak of those that "sleep in Jesus?" Does it not say, "We shall not all sleep, but we shall all be changed" (1 Cor. 15: 51)? Is not sleep unconsciousness? Yes, for the body; it is the body that sleeps; but you see, when my body falls asleep in Jesus, I leave the body. Oh, you say, I cannot understand that. "We walk by faith, not by sight." Faith believes the Book, and it says, "Absent from the body, present with the Lord." Notice how the apostle Paul speaks of this in the first chapter of Philippians. Here we see Paul in prison in Rome, waiting to be summoned be-

fore Nero, and he does not know what the outcome will be, whether he will be put to death or
set free, and he writes to the Philippian friends
and practically says, "Even if it were put up to
me to choose, I do not know which I would desire, whether to die a martyr's death or live a
little longer;" but as he meditates upon it he says,
"I really believe I would rather live a little longer
and preach Christ to people." "According to my
earnest expectation and my hope, that in nothing
I shall be ashamed, but that with all boldness, as
always, so now also Christ shall be magnified in
my body, whether it be by life, or by death" (ver.
20). Is not that a lovely expression? I want Christ
to be made large in my life; I do not want people
to think a great deal of Paul but of Christ. I want
to be used of God to make Christ seem great in
the eyes of men and women, "that Christ shall
be magnified in my body, whether it be by life,
or by death." If I can glorify Christ better by
living I want to live; if I can glorify Him better
by dying I want to die. The only thing is, I want
Christ to loom large in the eyes of people for
whom He died. "For me to live is Christ, and to
die is gain." There is only one reason to live, and
that is to glorify Jesus, and then if I die I will
go to be with Jesus, so that will be better. "But
if I live in the flesh, this is the fruit of my labor:
yet what I shall choose I wot not. For I am in a

strait betwixt two, having a desire to depart, and to be with Christ; which is far better: nevertheless to abide in the flesh is more needful for you." You cannot attach the thought of soul-sleep to that. If Paul thought of death as unconsciousness until the resurrection hour, he would have been in no dilemma. He would have said, "Since death is unconsciousness, I want to live as long as I can in order to preach Christ," but he says, No; it would be better to die because it would mean to be with Christ.

How did he know it would be far better? Well, you say, he was an inspired apostle and the Lord revealed it to him. That is true, but there is more than that. The apostle Paul at one time had been permitted to have a certain experience which proved to him beyond the peradventure of a doubt that it is far better to be with Christ in heaven than to live for Him on earth. People often say, "We do not know anything about heaven. Nobody has ever come back to tell us what it is like." But they are overlooking something. Our Lord Jesus Christ came down from heaven, and He says, "In My Father's house are many mansions (or abiding places)." Who are in those resting-places? All the saints who have gone on thus far. They are over yonder in the Father's house. And then we have the testimony of this very man, the apostle Paul, for when we turn to the twelfth chapter of this epistle, we find him relating for us a most remarkable experience which he passed through. When he went through this experience he was not conscious as to whether he was in the body or out of it. That is very interesting. Take our beloved friends who have died in Christ. We may sometimes think of them as in a very imperfect condition if their spirits are in heaven without the body, but Paul says, "If I was in the body I didn't know it, and if I was out of it I didn't miss it." So our dear friends over yonder do not miss their bodies; they are perfectly intelligent and perfectly happy; they are really people even if out of the body. They are in heaven, in the royal garden, in paradise. They hear unspeakable things which it is not possible for a man to utter. Are they able to commune one with another? Oh, yes. Our blessed Lord has told us, even before the work of the cross was accomplished, of that rich man in Hades, who looked across the great gulf and saw Lazarus and talked with Abraham, and among the lost the rich man was a personality, never to be rich again but to be poor. We read of "spirits of just men made perfect." What communion they have with each other over there! But the best of all is that they are with Christ.

PAUL'S THREE IMPELLING MOTIVES

✦ ✦ ✦

"Wherefore we labor, that, whether present or absent, we may be accepted of Him. For we must all appear before the judgment-seat of Christ; that every one may receive the things done in his body, according to that he hath done, whether it be good or bad. Knowing therefore the terror of the Lord, we persuade men; but we are made manifest unto God; and I trust also are made manifest in your consciences. For we commend not ourselves again unto you, but give you occasion to glory on our behalf, that ye may have somewhat to answer them which glory in appearance, and not in heart. For whether we be beside ourselves, it is to God: or whether we be sober, it is for your cause. For the love of Christ constraineth us" (2 Cor. 5:9-14).

✦ ✦ ✦

IN this section of the epistle the apostle Paul brings before us the three great motives that moved his heart as he went about through the world proclaiming the gospel of Christ. The first is this: He ever had it before his mind that all his work must soon be tested at the judgment-seat of Christ. What a solemn reflection it is for a Christian to remember that everything he says and everything he does as a believer is some day going to be examined by the

Lord Jesus, and he will be rewarded accordingly! This, of course, is an altogether different thing from the Christless soul standing before the Great White Throne to be judged for his sins. The judgment-seat of Christ refers to that review which will take place when our blessed Lord returns again and gathers all His own before Himself. He says, "Behold, I come quickly; and My reward is with Me, to give to every man according as his work shall be" (Rev. 22: 12). The Son of Man is like one who has gone into a far country, but has left to his servants certain responsibilities and given them certain talents, and says, "Occupy till I come." Then when He returns again He is going to examine all their work, and reward everything that was the result of His Holy Spirit's control over their lives.

Notice the way the apostle puts it here. "Wherefore we labor, that, whether present or absent, we may be accepted of Him." This word translated "labor" really means "are ambitious." It might be translated, "Wherefore we are ambitious, that, whether present or absent, we may be accepted of Him." The apostle uses this same word in two other places in his letters. In one instance he tells us that he is ambitious not to build on another man's foundation, but to preach the gospel in the regions beyond, a most worthy ambition. He was a true missionary. And then again, writing to the Thessalonian saints, he exhorts them to study to be quiet and to do their own business. That may be translated, "Be ambitious to mind your own business." That is a wonderful ambition. So many are ambitious to mind other folks' business that they do not have time for their own. "We are ambitious, that, whether present or absent"—those words refer back to the first part of this chapter where we read, "Absent from the body, present with the Lord." Now he says, "We are ambitious that whether present in the body or whether with the Lord, whether we live or die, that we should be accepted of Him."

In the epistle to the Ephesians he tells us that God has made us "accepted in the Beloved" (Eph. 1: 6). As believers we are all accepted *in* Christ, but here we find that he is urgently desirous of being accepted *of* Christ. Notice the difference. Accepted *in* Him—that is my standing. God sees me in Him, and Christ Jesus is made unto me wisdom, even righteousness, sanctification, and redemption. He is my perfection. I am complete in Him. But now I who already am complete in Him, who already have been accepted in Him, am to be exercised about being accepted *of* Him. Accepted of Him really means being well-pleasing to Him. You see, accepted *in* Him is my standing, accepted *of* Him has to do with my state. I wonder whether this is our ambition. Let us search our hearts and ask what our ambition really is. Is it to excel in some particular line for which you feel you are specially adapted? Is it to be thought well of by men and women like yourself? Or is it to be well-pleasing to the Lord, to have His approval?

I remember very well hearing Dr. G. Campbell Morgan say that a great crisis came into his life when he first gave up his place as a schoolmaster to become a minister of Christ. It was a very solemn moment when he was set apart to the work of the Lord, and when he got home that night and went into his room, he fell down on his knees before God, and he was sure he could hear the Lord saying to him, "Now, Morgan, you have been set apart definitely for the ministry of the Word. Do you want to be a great preacher, or do you want to be My servant?" His first thought was, "Oh, I want to be a great preacher; surely there is no more laudable ambition than that." But why should the Lord put it that way —"Do you want to be a great preacher, or do you want to be My servant?" And he said, "Why can I not be His servant, and a great preacher?" He went through a time of real soul-struggle, and then the thought came that it might be in the will of God that as a servant of Christ his ministry should be a very obscure one, and he cried, "O blessed Lord, I would rather be Thy servant than anything else!" And God not only made him His servant but a great preacher. Sometimes we fulfil our deepest ambition by foregoing our own desires and saying, "Lord, I want to be Thy servant; just take me, make me, break me, do what Thou wilt with me." You remember that through Jeremiah the Lord said to Baruch: "Seekest thou great things for thyself? Seek them not" (Jer. 45:5). So He says to every one of us, "Seekest thou great things for thyself? Seek them not." But what should we seek? To be well-pleasing unto Him, so that whatever niche He calls upon us to fill we may fill it to His glory, and this in view of the judgment-seat.

"For we must all appear before the judgment-seat of Christ; that every one may receive the things done in his body, according to that he hath done, whether it be good or bad." Have you ever as a Christian stopped to think of what a solemn thing it will be when your life's work is ended, when all further opportunity for witnessing for Christ on earth will have gone by forever, when you stand in your glorified body before His judgment-seat, and He will go back over all the way you have come, and will give His own estimate of all your service, of everything you have ever attempted to do for Him? Will He have to say at such a time, "You had a very won-

derfui opportunity to glorify Me, but you failed
because you were so self-occupied, you were so
much concerned about what people would think
of you, instead of being concerned about pleasing
Me; I will have to blot all that out, I cannot reward you for that, for there was too much self
in that service"? And then He will point to something else, maybe something you had forgotten
altogether, and He will say, "There! You thought
you failed in that; didn't you? You really thought
you blundered so dreadfully that your whole testimony amounted to nothing, but I was listening
and observing, and I knew that in that hour of
weakness your one desire was to glorify Me, and
though nobody applauded you I took note of it
and will reward you for it." What a joy it will
be to receive His approval in that day. If we
learn to live as Paul did with the judgment-seat
of Christ before us, we will not be men-pleasers,
but we will be Christ-pleasers.

Notice the next motive that stirred the apostle's
heart to Christian endeavor. "Knowing therefore
the terror of the Lord, we persuade men; but we
are made manifest unto God; and I trust also are
made manifest in your consciences." This, I
think, is a forgotten note in modern preaching in
many places. "The terror of the Lord." Is there
anything in God to be afraid of? Away back in
the seventies Theodore Parker preached a sermon

that was widely published entitled, "There is Nothing in God to Fear," and in some way or another that false note that he struck at that time went all over this land, and more or less had its influence upon thousands of preachers who read that eloquent sermon, and men came to the conclusion that there was nothing in God to fear, and so dropped the doctrine of eternal punishment for impenitent sinners. They forgot that the Bible said, "It is a fearful thing to fall into the hands of the living God" (Heb. 10: 31), and substituted a rosewater gospel of the fatherhood of God and the brotherhood of man, instead of the stern reality set forth in this Book. But there is something in God to fear, something that the Christless man may well fear, and that is God's hatred of iniquity. God is of purer eyes than to look upon sin; He cannot but judge iniquity. And so the apostle said, "Knowing therefore the terror of the Lord, we persuade men." As he thought of Christians having to answer for their behavior at the judgment-seat of Christ it at once brought home to his heart what a solemn thing it would be for unsaved men to face their sins at the great white throne. The apostle Peter says, "The time is come that judgment must begin at the house of God: and if it first begin at us, what shall the end be of them that obey not the gospel of God? And if the righteous scarcely be saved,

where shall the ungodly and the sinner appear?"
(1 Pet. 4: 17, 18). If our blessed Lord does not
overlook one thing in the lives of His beloved
people, but if everything is coming into the light
in that day, what will it be for Christless men
to have all their sins made manifest at His judg-
ment-bar, and to meet a just and awful doom?
As Paul went out to this poor Christless world
he realized he was going to men that were lost,
not merely in danger of being lost some day, but
lost here and now in this life. But he had a gospel for lost men, "The Son of Man is come to
seek and to save that which was lost" (Luke 19:
10), and so he went to men with Christ. He did
not go out to glorify himself or to get a certain
reputation among men.

He says, "We commend not ourselves again
unto you, but give you occasion to glory on our
behalf, that ye may have somewhat to answer
them which glory in appearance, and not in
heart." When you find men who profess to be
servants of Christ glorying in outward appearance, Paul says, you can contrast our behavior
with theirs—we are made the very offscouring of
the earth for Christ's sake and are not seeking
man's applause, we are seeking the approval of
the Lord Jesus Christ. There were those who
said of Paul, The man is insane; it is not natural
that any man should be actuated by such motives

as these; it is not natural for a man to live a life such as this. Very well, he says, "Whether we be beside ourselves, it is to God: or whether we be sober, it is for your cause." We are not even concerned about insisting that we are sane; we are not even concerned about insisting that our words are words of sobriety; we leave that to God to judge. We proclaim the message in dependence on the Holy Spirit, and are not concerned at all about man's approval or disapproval. Our business is to glorify Christ and to seek to save the lost. This is the ideal preacher of the Word. I never read words like these but I feel so condemned in my own conscience that I hardly know how to talk to other people. I can detect in my own heart so much pride, so much human ambition, so much selfishness, so much that is different from what was found in the Lord Jesus Christ, that I have to bow before Him and tell Him I am so unworthy to be His servant, and yet to plead with Him for Jesus' sake to use one, even though unworthy, who at least has some little desire to see poor sinners brought to a saving knowledge of God's beloved Son.

It is always comforting to know that everything that God has done in this world, He has done through imperfect instruments. He has never had a perfect instrument. I do not think of Jesus as an instrument, He was God—"God was in Christ, reconciling the world unto Himself" (2 Cor. 5: 19)—but I am thinking of His prophets, His preachers, pastors, evangelists, teachers, apostles, they are all imperfect. A Peter denied his Lord, even a John and a James were ambitious to sit one on the right hand and one on the left hand of the Lord in His kingdom, and a Paul made a mistake at the last and insisted on going up to Jerusalem against the voice of the Spirit. Even the best of God's servants have failed, and yet how gracious of Him to use them. He uses the message they bring, the truth they proclaim. He will deal with His servants Himself about their failure, but He will use the message when Christ is lifted up.

Now notice the last of these three impelling motives. Paul says, "For the love of Christ constraineth us." I stop here in the middle of a sentence, for these words in themselves are enough; they complete our theme. What are Paul's three impelling motives? First, a realization of the fact that we must all stand before the judgment-seat of Christ; second, a recognition of the fact that men are lost and exposed to the judgment of God; and third, the love of Christ constraining, that all-conquering love that laid hold of the heart of proud, haughty, self-righteous, cruel Saul of Tarsus, that religious zealot who went forth with a heart filled with hatred for the name of Jesus, seeking to bind those that loved Him, to cast them in prison and compel them to blaspheme, in fact to put them to death if they did not renounce Christ. There he was, hastening on to Damascus with no thought in his soul that the time would ever come when he would be the greatest preacher of the gospel which he was then seeking to destroy, that this world should ever know. He fell to the ground, a light brighter than the sun shone round about him, and he heard a voice from the glory exclaiming in sweet accents, "Saul, Saul, why persecutest thou Me? It is hard for thee to kick against the pricks." And trembling and astonished he exclaimed, "Who art Thou, Lord?" And the answer came back, "I am Jesus whom thou persecutest. But rise, and stand upon thy feet: for I have appeared unto thee for this purpose, to make thee a minister and a witness, both of these things which thou hast seen, and of those things in the which I will appear unto thee, to open their eyes, and to turn them from darkness to light, and from the power of Satan unto God, that they may receive forgiveness of sins, and inheritance among them which are sanctified by faith that is in Me" (Acts 26:14-18). And in that one glorious moment the darkness disappeared from Saul's heart, the veil was torn away, his eyes were opened, Christ filled the vision of his soul, and henceforth he could say, "The love of Christ constraineth me." That is what made him the man that he was, actuated, motivated by divine love. Do you know that love? Have you too been laid hold of by the love of Christ? Then, may you go forth to make Him known to others.

WHY CHRIST DIED

✓ ✓ ✓

"For the love of Christ constraineth us; because we thus judge, that if One died for all, then were all dead: and that He died for all, that they which live should not henceforth live unto themselves, but unto Him which died for them, and rose again. Wherefore henceforth know we no man after the flesh: yea, though we have known Christ after the flesh, yet now henceforth know we Him no more. Therefore if any man be in Christ, he is a new creature: old things are passed away; behold, all things are become new. And all things are of God, who hath reconciled us to Himself by Jesus Christ, and hath given to us the ministry of reconciliation; to wit, that God was in Christ, reconciling the world unto Himself, not imputing their trespasses unto them; and hath committed unto us the word of reconciliation. Now then we are ambassadors for Christ, as though God did beseech you by us: we pray you in Christ's stead, be ye reconciled to God. For He hath made Him to be sin for us, who knew no sin; that we might be made the righteousness of God in Him" (2 Cor. 5: 14-21).

✓ ✓ ✓

IN this section of the epistle Paul brings before us in a very clear, definite way, the supreme reason for the death of our Lord Jesus Christ. We see not merely One who loved God His Father and loved the truth, and was therefore

willing to die as a martyr for truth, but we see
One who took His place as a vicarious sacrifice,
suffering instead of others, bearing the judgment
that sinners deserved in order that they might be
delivered from that judgment, and that they
might be brought into a new creation, a new relationship with God altogether, and then might
go forth with hearts aflame with love for Christ
to carry the story of His grace to all men everywhere. This is the way that Christianity has
been propagated down through the centuries.
Mohammedanism was propagated by the sword.
Its advocates said, "Accept the religion of Mo-
hammed or die." Other systems have been ad-
vanced by appeal to selfish interests. But Christianity has been propagated down through all the
centuries in the power of the Holy Spirit,
through the setting forth of the death, the burial,
and the resurrection of our Lord Jesus Christ,
calling upon men through Christ to be reconciled
to God, and what marvels this gospel has
wrought!

The apostle says, "'The love of Christ constraineth us." Spurred on by his own sense of
that mighty, all-conquering love, he went out into
a world of sinners to win men for Christ, "because," he tells us, "we thus judge, that if One
died for all, then were all dead." That is, mankind as a whole was under sentence of death, that

came in with the fall of the first man. Adam
stood there before God as our federal head. He
was the head of the old creation, and that old
creation was on trial in Adam. God said to him,
"Thou shalt not eat of it: for in the day that
thou eatest thereof, dying thou shalt die" (Gen.
2: 17, *Margin*). Adam deliberately disobeyed
this command of God, and he fell under sentence
of death, and of course took the entire human
race down with him, for all were represented in
him as he stood before God. And so all mankind
now are in the place of death.

I have sometimes tried to illustrate it like this.
Think of the top of this reading-desk as repre-
senting paradise, that place in which God put
man when He first created him. This hymn-book
which I hold erect on the desk may speak to you
of Adam as the head of the race. There our
first father stood in the position of responsibility
before God, a sinless man in Eden. Had he been
obedient, he would never have come under the
sentence of death, but through disobedience he
fell under that sentence. Sinning against God
he went down into the place of death; just as I
drop this book from the top of the reading-desk
to the platform, you may think of Adam falling
from that place of sinlessness, where he was free
of all condemnation, down into the place of death
because of sin. And mark, every person who

has ever come into the world since, has come into the world down there in the place of death. Not one has come into the world up here on this plane of sinlessness. Therefore, all are dead, as God looks at men, dead in trespasses and sin. But now think of our Lord Jesus Christ. He comes into the world as the sinless One; He stands not only on the plane where Adam was, the plane of innocence, but He is absolutely holy. But He has come to save men. He cannot find any men on this plane of sinlessness; He does not find men enjoying life and fellowship with God. Where does He have to go to find them? He goes down into the place of death where man is. "And that He died for all." Because men were dead He went down into death, and now He brings believers up with Him in resurrection life. To put them here on the same plane where Adam was before he fell? Oh, no; to lift them infinitely higher, that they may be made members of a new creation of which He is the exalted Head in heaven: "He hath raised us up together, and made us sit together in heavenly places in Christ Jesus" (Eph. 2: 6).

"If Christ died for all, then were all dead." No man has title to life in himself, but Christ died for all "that they which live," those who have put their trust in Him, those to whom He has spoken life, now possessors of eternal life through faith, "should not henceforth live unto themselves, but unto Him which died for them, and rose again." Why did Christ die? Not only that we should be delivered from death and judgment, but that we should be brought up from our state of death into newness of life. Now our redeemed lives should be devoted to Him that we should live henceforth to the glory of God alone. And so we now look out upon the world through altogether different eyes from those we used when we belonged to it. When men of the world, we made much of the flesh and all that was linked with it. We thought of men as great, or as rich, or as powerful, talented or able, as superior one to another. Some men we despised because they were poor and ignorant and degraded, with little intelligence, and less talented, but now all that is changed. "Henceforth know we no man after the flesh." We look out now upon this world, not thinking of the different distinctions between man and man, but as seeing a world of sinners for whom Christ died, and we realize that all men, whether rich or poor, foolish or wise, whether barbarian or civilized, whether morons or highly talented, are dear to the heart of God, that "God so loved the world, that He gave His only begotten Son, that whosoever believeth in Him should not perish, but have everlasting life" (John 3: 16). So, in touch with Christ Himself,

we are prepared to suffer, to give, to deny ourselves, we are prepared to die, if need be, in order
to bring others to a saving knowledge of this redemption which means so much to us.

"Yea," the apostle continues, "though we have
known Christ after the flesh, yet now henceforth
know we Him no more." He is not saying that
he personally ever did know Christ after the
flesh, but uses the "we" here in order to take in
others with him who were actually acquainted
with our Lord when here on earth. He is telling
us that it is not the incarnate Christ with whom
we are linked, it is the resurrected Christ. In-
carnation apart from His death would never have
saved one poor sinner. We do not think of Him
merely as the promised Messiah of Israel, as a
great prophet sent of God, as the greatest of all
ethical and spiritual teachers, but look far beyond
the cross and the grave into the glory, and see
Him there exalted at God's right hand, a Prince
and a Saviour, and we go to men in His name
to proclaim remission of sins, knowing that when
they trust Him, when they believe the message,
"If any man be in Christ, it is new creation."
He, the risen, exalted Christ, has now become the
Head of an altogether new creation. Who belong
to that new creation? All who, though once in
death because of sin, have now been quickened
into newness of life through faith in the Lord

Jesus Christ. That is, we enter that new creation by being born again.

Does any one say, "How may I know definitely whether I belong to that new creation or not?" Listen to what our Lord Himself says, "Verily, verily, I say unto you, He that heareth My word, and believeth on Him that sent Me, hath everlasting life, and shall not come into condemnation; but is passed from death unto life" (John 5:24). I am very fond of the Roman Catholic translation of that verse, the translation that you will find in the Rheims-Douay Version of the Bible. There you read, "Amen, amen, I say unto you, He who hears My word, and believes Him who sent Me, has eternal life, and comes not into judgment; but is passed out of death into life." Is not that a wonderful translation? Do you sense the meaning of it? The Word of God speaks with that double affirmation which is equivalent to the divine oath: "Amen, amen, truly, truly, I say unto you, if you hear My word, and you believe Him that sent Me, you have eternal life, and shall not come into judgment; but you are passed out of death into life." That is, if you receive the gospel message in your heart, you have everlasting life. It is not something you have to work for, or pray for, it is something that God gives instantaneously when you put your trust in the One who is revealed in the gospel. You will never come into judgment, but already God sees you as having passed out of that condition of death into life, and thus linked with Christ as the Head of the new creation.

"If any man be in Christ, it is new creation." And in this new creation "old things are passed away, behold, all things are become new." We have done with our old state and condition. The old creation fell in Adam; the new creation stands in Christ; and once in Him we are in Him forever. The moment you put your trust in Him God links you up with Him. If Christ fails, the new creation will go down, as the old one did when its head fell. But Christ will never fail. Christ is already seated on the throne of God in heaven, and we are linked with Him, and there in this new creation "all things are of God." Do not try to read into this what some New Thought advocates seek to read into it. They will take a statement like this and will tell us it means that there is nothing evil in the universe, and so we must not even think of Satan as evil. Satan, they tell us, is only the personification of our wrong thoughts, but we know from the Word of God that our "adversary the devil, as a roaring lion, walketh about, seeking whom he may devour" (1 Pet. 5: 8). There is a great deal of evil in this universe, but it all belongs to the old creation. The apostle is speaking of the new creation, and it is in the new creation that "all things are of God, who hath reconciled us to Himself by Jesus Christ." This reconciliation is even more than justification. When we come to Christ, all all our sins are forgiven; more than that, we are justified from all things. God looks upon us as though we had never sinned at all. Justification is the sentence of the judge in favor of the prisoner, it is God saying, "I declare this man not guilty," No wonder the apostle tells us, "Being justified by faith, we have peace with God through our Lord Jesus Christ" (Rom. 5:1). Reconciliation goes a step farther; it is not only that our sins are forgiven and that divine justice has nothing against us, but it is that He has received us as His own to His loving heart, and we are reconciled to God and we joy in Him.

In our unconverted state we would not have thought such a thing possible. We were happy only when we could get God out of our minds, but now we find our joy in the Lord. It was not the life merely of Jesus that reconciled us, but we were reconciled to God by the death of His Son. God in His love and grace had come out to seek us in the Person of the Lord Jesus, and actually in Christ went to the cross and settled the sin question for us. The Lord Jesus loved us and gave Himself for us, and that broke down all the enmity and won our hearts to Him. Henceforth we are reconciled to the God from whom at one time we turned away.

Now He has given to us a ministry, "the ministry of reconciliation." This ministry of reconciliation is God's call to lost men everywhere to come to Him with all their sins, with all their griefs, with all their burdens, and be reconciled to Him. Mark, it is not that God has to be reconciled to us.

God never had one hard thought toward me. Sinner, He has never had one hard thought toward you. You have had hard thoughts toward Him, and because of that you have taken it for granted that of course God felt the same toward you, but He loves you in spite of all your sin and folly and iniquity. God's heart goes out toward you in love. Jesus did not die in order to enable God to love sinners, but He died *because* God loves sinners. "God so loved that He gave." He so loved a world of sinners "that He gave His only begotten Son, that whosoever believeth in Him should not perish, but have everlasting life." And so it is not God who needs to be reconciled to us, but we as sinners need reconciliation to Him. If you have never yet turned to Him, you need to go to Him, and when you realize something of His grace toward you, you will be reconciled to Him. It is a wonderful thing when all enmity disappears and you can joy in the

Lord and rejoice in the God of your salvation.
This is reconciliation.

But in the next verses the apostle unfolds this
ministry of reconciliation. He says, "And hath
given to us the ministry of reconciliation; namely,
that God was in Christ, reconciling the world
unto Himself." The Lord Jesus Christ was no
ordinary man; He was not simply the best of
men; but He was God manifest in flesh. "God
was in Christ reconciling the world unto Himself;" that is, God in Christ was going out after
men to try to win them back. They had gone
away from Him, trampling on His goodness,
spurning His love, actually assailing His righteousness, but here God in Christ goes out after
them, pleads with them to return to God, offers
to forgive them, to put away all their sins and
make them His own. "God was in Christ, reconciling the world unto Himself, not imputing their
trespasses unto them." Christ did not come to
charge man's sins against him but to pay man's
debt. We read of that poor woman in the eighth
chapter of John's Gospel and get such a conception of the cruelty and hardness of man's heart.
She had fallen into a heinous sin, and they dragged her into the temple where the people were
gathered, and pointed the finger of scorn at her
as she stood there with downcast eyes, trembling,
overwhelmed with shame. They told the story of

her sin and degradation, but what did Jesus do? He stooped down and with His finger wrote on the ground. Why did He do that? In Jeremiah it is written, "They that depart from Me shall be written on the earth" (Jer. 17: 13). They were saying of this woman, "What a sinner she is, how vile, how guilty!" but Jesus, by His very act, is saying, "You are all guilty; you are all to be written in the earth. From dust you came, and to dust you go because of sin," and then lifting Himself up He said, "He that is without sin among you let him first cast a stone at her," and then stooped to the dust again. I think that second going down to the dust suggested that He Himself was about to descend into the place of death to bring poor sinners up to this sphere of life, but as He wrote again upon the dust they turned and went away, from the eldest even until the least. The oldest rascal there, with all his piety, knew he had sins enough to sink his soul to the depths of hell, and the next, until the youngest was gone, and the woman was left alone with Jesus, and of course the multitude standing around. And when Jesus looked up He said, "Hath no man condemned thee?" She said, "No man, Lord." By that term, "Lord," she expressed her faith in Him, for "no man can call Jesus Lord but by the Holy Ghost." And He said, "Neither do I condemn thee: go, and sin no more" (Jno. 8:7-11).

"Not imputing their trespasses unto them." The Son of Man came not to condemn the world but to save the world. What! you say, does He not condemn a sin like that? Does He make light of uncleanness and unchastity and licentiousness? No; but for all that sin He was going to the cross. The condemnation was to fall on Him, and because He was to bear that poor woman's sin, when she trusted in Him, He could send her away uncondemned. "God was in Christ, reconciling the world unto Himself, not imputing their trespasses unto them, and hath committed unto us the word of reconciliation." He has intrusted the administration of the gospel message to us; and Paul says, "We are ambassadors for Christ." We go to men on God's behalf, "as though God did beseech you by us: we pray you in Christ's stead, be ye reconciled to God." How can we be reconciled to God? We may be ashamed of our sins, we may grieve over our past, but will not sin ever remain, will it not ever rise up between our souls and God in spite of our deepest repentance? No; because in the cross that question has been fully met to the divine satisfaction. God has made Christ to be sin for us. "He hath made Him to be sin for us, who knew no sin; that we might become the righteousness of God in Him." And upon the cross Christ took the sinner's place, He was treated as though guilty of all the sin

and iniquity and unrighteousness of the ages. He
was there as the great Sin Offering.

> "On Him almighty vengeance fell,
>   That would have sunk a world to hell;
>   He bore it for a chosen race,
>   And thus becomes our Hiding-Place."

And because He, the sinless One, has died in the
place of sinners, we, the sinful, may enter into
life, may become the righteousness of God in
Him.

This last verse of our chapter epitomizes the
deepest meaning of the cross. It shows the One
who was sinless inwardly and outwardly, enduring the wrath of God which we deserved. Our
sins put Him on the cross. But, having settled
the sin-question to the divine satisfaction, He has
been raised from the dead and seated as the glorified Man at God's right hand. There on the
throne He is our righteousness. The Father sees
every believer in Him, free from all condemnation, made the display of the righteousness of
God in Him. He Himself is our righteousness.
We are complete in Him. God is satisfied and
our consciences are at peace. What a salvation
is this!

THE IDEAL MINISTER OF CHRIST

✐ ✐ ✐

"We then, as workers together with him, beseech you also that ye receive not the grace of God in vain. (For He saith, I have heard thee in a time accepted, and in the day of salvation have I succored thee: behold, now is the accepted time; behold, now is the day of salvation.) Giving no offence in any thing, that the ministry be not blamed: but in all things approving ourselves as the ministers of God, in much patience, in afflictions, in necessities, in distresses, in stripes, in imprisonments, in tumults, in labors, in watchings, in fastings; by pureness, by knowledge, by longsuffering, by kindness, by the Holy Ghost, by love unfeigned, by the word of truth, by the power of God, by the armor of righteousness on the right hand and on the left, by honor and dishonor, by evil report and good report: as deceivers, and yet true; as unknown, and yet well known; as dying, and, behold, we live; as chastened, and not killed: as sorrowful, yet always rejoicing; as poor, yet making many rich; as having nothing, and yet possessing all things" (2 Cor. 6: 1-10). ✐ ✐ ✐

THIS is the standard that the Spirit of God sets up for every servant of Christ, and is that at which every true "minister of God" should aim. You will notice the apostle speaks of such as fellow-workers with the rest of His people. "We then, as workers together with him, beseech you also that ye receive not the grace of God in vain." The New Testament minister of Christ, the scriptural pastor, evangelist, or teacher, is not one who lords it over the consciences of God's people, but he is a fellow-worker with them. The italicized words, "with him," which may suggest workers together *with God* are not really found in the original. The apostle is not exactly saying, "We are fellow-workers with God," for we are under God as our Master, but we who are members of the Church, and those of us who have particular responsibility, are fellow-workers, we are laborers together for the blessing of the whole Body of Christ and for the evangelization of a lost world. Addressing this church, the apostle says, "We beseech you also that ye receive not the grace of God in vain." Christians have been richly blessed; God has lavished His goodness upon us. What response are we making to the love of His heart? To receive His great goodness, to glory in salvation by grace, and yet to live carnal, worldly lives is indeed to "receive the grace of God in vain." Let there be on our part a constant response of loving devotion to Him who has so graciously accepted us in the Beloved.

"For He saith, I have heard thee in a time accepted, and in the day of salvation have I succored thee: behold, now is the accepted time: behold, now is the day of salvation." The apostle quotes this passage from the Old Testament to remind us how God has taken us up when poor sinners and has made us His own. But I cannot pass the last part of this quotation without reminding any who are out of Christ that this message of salvation is still going out to a lost world and to all men everywhere. God is saying, "Behold, now is the accepted time; behold, now is the day of salvation." If you are still in your sins, still out of Christ, there is no reason why you should go on even for one more day, for one hour, even for one minute, refusing the salvation God is offering, or fearing to appropriate it lest it might not yet be God's time to save. It is ever God's time: "Now is the accepted time; behold, now is the day of salvation." The moment you are ready to turn to God as a poor, lost, needy sinner, that moment He is ready to receive and to save and to grant you His forgiveness and to make you His child. This verse really comes in parenthetically. In the verses that follow the apostle sets forth the ideal minister of Christ.

In the first place, he must be careful of his own personal behavior that he may not stumble another. "Giving no offence in any thing." By the term "offence" he does not mean hurting people's feelings. It is quite impossible for any servant of Christ to behave himself so as never to hurt the feelings of someone. It is impossible to so speak, to so act that one can forever be free from hurting people's feelings. Some people carry their feelings on their sleeves all the time.

If you do not shake hands with them, you probably intended to slight them. If you do, you hurt them, forgetting they have rheumatism. If you stop to speak with them, you are interrupting them. If you do not, you are "high-hatting" them. If you write them a letter, they are sure you want to get their money. If you do not, you are neglecting them. If you visit them, you are bothering them. If you do not, it shows you have no interest in the flock. It is impossible to please everyone, but when the apostle says, "Giving no offence," he means so behaving yourself that no one can point to you and say, "That man's ways are such that I lose confidence in the salvation that he professes." The minister of Christ must first of all be a regenerated man, and then a man walking in the power of the Holy Spirit, "giving no occasion of stumbling in anything, that the ministry be not blamed. But in all things approving ourselves as the ministers of God, in much patience." How much patience the minister of Christ needs!

The apostle then gives us three series of nines. First, he gives us in nine different expressions the testing of the minister of Christ. He is to manifest much patience in *affliction*. He is not to expect to be above affliction; it is the common lot of God's people in this scene. And the minister of Christ must share with the rest in *neces-*

sity. He is not to expect to live in luxury while others are often distressed. I have been thankful for experiences that God has given me in difficult pioneer days in Christian work. They enable me to enter into the feelings of others who are in deep need. I have often known what it was to pull up my belt one notch for breakfast, and another for lunch, and another for supper. The longest time I went without food and kept on preaching, was three days and three nights, and yet by the grace of God I was enabled to preach three times a day during those three days and nights. I happened to be in a place where I had no money, and God's people thought I lived by faith and they let me do it, but nothing came in for food. I have often thanked God for those days, for I have found out how God could sustain a man altogether without food. I shall never forget when on the morning of the fourth day I thought I would stay in bed for breakfast, and then I saw a letter slipped under my door. I opened it and found these words, "Inclosed is an expression of Christian fellowship," and there was a ten-dollar bill. I went out and enjoyed the best breakfast that I ever remember having in my life. Hunger whets the appetite. I fancy there are very few who have trod the path of faith who have not known these things.

And then the Christian minister is to approve

himself in *distresses*, and if he cannot find anything otherwise to distress him, he will always
find someone to help him along. In Paul's day
ministers had to pass through what few of us
are called upon to pass through these days. "In
stripes, in *imprisonments*, in *tumults*, in *labors*,
in *watchings*, in *fastings*." Here you have the
training of the minister. He is to learn his lessons in the school of affliction that he may able
to enter into and sympathize with the people of
God in their afflictions.

And then in verses 6, 7 we read of nine char-
acteristics that should mark him out as a man
of God. He is to be characterized by *pureness*.
The minister of Christ is to be above anything
like uncleanness of life or thought, he is to be
marked by that purity that characterized the
Lord Jesus Christ. And then "by *knowledge*."
It is his responsibility to become acquainted
with the things of God and with other branches
of useful knowledge that may help him to minister to people in their various states of heart
and mind, for he should be Christ's servant to
the fullest possible extent. Then he must be
marked "by *longsuffering*," not readily provoked.
In fact, the apostle tells us, that where love con-
trols the heart, one is not easily provoked.
Nothing so shows a man out of fellowship with
God as a bad temper. A bad-tempered minister

will never be a real testimony for Christ. Then, "by *kindness.*" And how one fails in this, how little he rises to this ideal! Men and women long to find those who have a tender, kindly interest in them. And this should characterize the pastor.

But next we read, "By the *Holy Ghost.*" He is to be a man not only indwelt by the Holy Ghost but filled with the Spirit of God, living in the power of the Spirit, and so ministering by the Spirit. I have prayed hundreds of times, and I still pray, "God keep me from ever being able to preach except in the power of the Holy Spirit of God." I would rather be smitten dumb than mock God and mock the people to whom I speak, by simply standing up to give them my own vain thoughts instead of the mind of God in the energy of His Spirit. And then again we read, "By *love unfeigned.*" A love that is genuine, not put on, that is not pretended but is real, because implanted in the heart by the Spirit of God. "By the *word of truth.*" The minister of Christ must know his Bible, and preach the Bible by the power of God, which only comes as one draws from Him in secret before appearing in public. "By the *armor of righteousness* on the right hand and on the left." That is, right living, right doing.

And then in closing this description of the ideal minister we have in verses 8 to 10, nine paradoxes which are all to be seen in the man of God.

"By *honor and dishonor.*" Some may approve
and some may disapprove, but he is to keep the
even tenor of his way. "By *evil report and good
report.*" Some may say wicked, unkind things
about him, but he is not to retaliate. Others may
over-praise him, but he is not to be lifted up but
to go on in dependence on the Lord. "As *deceivers, and yet true.*" Men may claim that he knows
not whereof he speaks, but he is to give his message knowing it to be the very Word of God. "As
unknown, and yet well known." How little the
minister of Christ counts for in the great world
outside, and yet how much he may mean to the
people of God. I remember well how stirred I
was when our late beloved brother, Dr. R. A.
Torrey, passed away. I was in New York and
I picked up a newspaper, and there saw a little
two-inch item saying that Dr. R. A. Torrey had
died, and in the same paper there was a column-
and-a-half telling of the death of a moving-picture
actor on the same date. But when I picked up a
Christian journal a little later, I found column
after column telling of Dr. Torrey, and there was
no mention of the actor! It makes all the difference which crowd you belong to. "As *dying, and,
behold, we live.*" The apostle says, "I die daily,"
and then again, "We which live are alway delivered unto death for Jesus' sake" (chap. 4: 11).
And then, "As *chastened, and not killed*"—as

patiently enduring divine discipline and yet not
killed. "As *sorrowful, yet always rejoicing.*"
How can a man be sorrowful and always be rejoicing? No man can look around upon a world
like this without sorrow if he possesses the Spirit
of Christ. Yet we are made to rejoice as we
think of the goodness of the Lord. "As *poor, yet
making many rich.*" I have heard of very few
servants of Christ possessed of much of this
world's wealth. They go through life giving not
only their testimony but of their means to bless
and help others, and die at last leaving little behind them, and yet if they have been the means
of bringing many souls to Christ and building
up His people in the truth, what a privilege that
is, for they have been making many rich. "As
having nothing, and yet possessing all things."
The minister of Christ surrenders in a large
measure his right to a place in this world, to the
honor of this world, to the wealth of this world.
But though surrendering it all, though it seems he
may be literally throwing away his life, in Christ
he has everything. This is the ideal minister of
Christ. To what extent do we who are engaged
in the work of the Lord measure up to it? Let
us test ourselves by these verses, and seek by
grace to manifest those things that the Holy
Spirit here puts before us. Then our hearers will
indeed realize that we have been with Jesus and
learned of Him!

SEPARATION FROM EVIL

✓ ✓ ✓

"O ye Corinthians, our mouth is open unto you, our heart is enlarged. Ye are not straitened in us, but ye are straitened in your own bowels. Now for a recompence in the same, (I speak as unto my children,) be ye also enlarged. Be ye not unequally yoked together with unbelievers: for what fellowship hath righteousness with unrighteousness? and what communion hath light with darkness? And what concord hath Christ with Belial? or what part hath he that believeth with an infidel? And what agreement hath the temple of God with idols? for ye are the temple of the living God; as God hath said, I will dwell in them, and walk in them; and I will be their God, and they shall be My people. Wherefore come out from among them, and be ye separate, saith the Lord, and touch not the unclean thing; and I will receive you, and will be a Father unto you, and ye shall be My sons and daughters, saith the Lord Almighty" (2 Cor. 6: 11-18).

✓ ✓ ✓

ALL down through the ages since God has been working redemptively in delivering men from sin, from its guilt and its power, Satan has been seeking in every possible way to thwart that work, and although Calvary has demonstrated the fact that he is already a defeated adversary, yet he still persists in trying

to injure by all means in his power everything
that is of God. You will find as you read both
Testaments, that in every instance when God begins a new testimony Satan seeks to destroy it
by persecution. He stirs up the hearts of those
who hate God and hate His Word to work injury
upon those who love Him and love the Scriptures.
This was particularly true in the beginning of
the history of the Church of God. Persecution
broke out first in Jerusalem, and then spread
through the world, finally centering itself in
Rome, and for two hundred awful years the devil
did everything possible to destroy the Church of
God by stirring up the hatred of men and women
throughout the entire Roman empire, so that
literally hundreds of thousands of Christian men,
women, and children were martyred for Christ's
sake. But down through the ages it has been
demonstrated, as Augustine said, "The blood of
the martyrs is the seed of the Church." Satan
always finds that persecution is utterly unable
to destroy the testimony of God.

And then the enemy of souls works in another
way. He persecutes, he destroys, he puts God's
people to death, gives them to realize the bitter
enmity of the world, and when that will not keep
folk from coming to Christ, nor keep the Church
from witnessing for Christ, he turns the tables,
and seeks to become in some sense the patron of

Christianity. He endeavors to render the testimony of the Church innocuous by amalgamation with the world. It is in this way that Israel fell. As long as Israel remained a separated people they had a testimony for God in the world, but when they followed after the idolatry of the nations, when they made marriages with the heathen, they lost their testimony, and so God set them to one side. They were of no further use as a witness in the world. It has been the same with the Church throughout the centuries. As long as the Church walked in holy separation from the world it has been a power for God, sinners have been convicted, and anxious ones have been saved. Whole nations have been stirred by a separated, devoted, godly people, but just as soon as the Church has listened to the suggestions of the enemy, coming now in the guise of a friend, and has given her fair hand to the world, has amalgamated with the world, at once her testimony has been annulled, she has ceased to be of any real account for God in this scene. In the Word of God we find the importance of separation from evil stressed. If we would really count for the Lord we need to remember this, for the professing Church all about us has become contaminated to a great extent by the spirit of the world. How often we find ourselves going after the ways of the world, and very often we dress and behave just like the world, and indulge in the same things that the world indulges in, and so lose our power with souls.

The story is told of a young woman, brought up in a very careful Christian home, who when she went away to college was persuaded by some nominal Christians that if she would have any influence with her fellow-students she would have to let down the bars a little bit. So at last she was persuaded to learn to dance, and she later went to the college prom. There on the floor she was dancing with a young man, and as she danced she said to herself, "I am doing this in order to let people see that I am not narrow, to let folk see that I can meet them on their own ground, and I must remember to bear witness for Christ here." And so as the dance went on she tried to say a little word, but her partner did not know what it was all about. As he led her back to a seat she said, "What I am anxious to know is, Are you a Christian?"

He looked at her and said, "Good gracious, no. You are not; are you?"

"Oh, yes," she said; "I am."

"Well, what on earth are you doing here, then?"

She realized at once that even the world has a high standard for a Christian. The world expects a Christian to walk in separation from it. It will do what it can to get the Christian to lower his standard, but always despises him when he does lower it.

I was having meetings in a church in San Jose, California, some years ago. One night the leader announced that a certain young lady would sing a solo. She was very beautiful, and had a carefully-trained, well-modulated voice, and sang very nicely. The title of the song was, "Jesus Satisfies." I was quite moved by it myself, and hoped others were. At the close of the meeting I asked any anxious ones to meet me at the front or to remain in their seats. I noticed a young woman sitting by herself, and so I went down to speak with her. I said, "Are you anxious about your soul?"

She looked at me and said, "Well, yes, and no. I was anxious; I came to this meeting with the thought that I would like to become a Christian, but if ever I become a Christian I want to be a different one from Miss So-and-So," and she gave the name of the young lady who had sung the solo.

"Oh," I said; "you are acquainted with the young lady?"

"Oh, yes."

"But you don't like her particularly?"

"Oh," she said, "she is my best friend."

"But what do you mean, then?"

"Well," she said, "it is just this. I believe a

Christian ought to live a different life from a worldling. I am a worldling, and I do not profess to be anything else. I have been trying to find satisfaction in the world; I confess I have never found it, but my friend, Miss So-and-So, got up and sang, 'Jesus Satisfies,' and that is a lie; He doesn't satisfy her. She professes to be a Christian, and she often tells me I ought to be a Christian, but when I go to the theater I always find her there, when I go to the ball I find her there, when I go to a card-party she is there, when I go into anything of the world, she is always there. What difference is there between her and myself? The only difference I can see is that she professes to have something which I do not profess to possess, but it does not do anything for her. Her life is just like mine."

What could I as the preacher say? I talked to the young woman, and tried to show her that no matter how Christians fail Christ abides and He never fails, but she got up and went out unsaved.

The Christian's power comes from a separated life, and a separated life results from being filled with the Holy Spirit of God. As you walk in obedience to the Word of God the Spirit of God fills you, and thus you go out to live in the world to the glory of the Lord Jesus. One of the troubles of the Corinthians was this, there were many Christians there, but they were trying to give their friends the idea that Christianity was a very liberal thing, and so were amalgamating with the world. And the apostle says, "O ye Corinthians, our mouth is open unto you. We do not want to find fault with you, we do not want you to think that we are narrow and bound, and do not sympathize with you. We love you, our hearts go out to you; we put these things before you because we love you." Christians, and specially at times some of our dear young Christians, imagine that when those of us who are interested in their souls speak to them seriously and earnestly about the folly of worldliness, and try to guide them in the path of devotion to Christ, that it is because we have grown older, that we do not sympathize with youth and do not understand their problems. Let me say, "You are not straitened in us." Our hearts are really concerned about you, "but you are straitened in your own bowels," you are narrowing your own life by worldliness. You do not realize this, you think you are enjoying life because you are letting down the bars, but you are not. You are not getting out of Christ what you might, and you are not getting out of your Christian life what you might, if you were more devoted to the One whom you call Lord. Your life is narrow and straitened because of inconsistency. This was true of the Corinthians, and this is true of many today.

Paul tells them, "I want you to be enlarged, to get the best out of life, to enjoy to the fullest what Christ has for you," and in order that this may be, he gives them a most earnest exhortation: "Be ye not unequally yoked together with unbelievers." What does he mean by that? The reference is, of course, to the passage in Deuteronomy 22:10. God said to His people, who were an agricultural people, "Thou shalt not plow with an ox and an ass together." The ox was a clean beast. It could be offered in sacrifice and its flesh used for food. The ass was an unclean beast. It could not be offered to the Lord and its flesh could not be eaten. And God said, You are not to take these two and yoke them together, even for service, for they do not belong together. And so He says to the Christians, You cannot expect to glorify Me if linked up with an ungodly man or woman, even for service. "Be ye not unequally yoked together with unbelievers." The passage applies to Church relationship, to things in society where you have to be in fellowship with unsaved people, to being in business with unsaved folk. Many a Christian has found out to his sorrow that he made his mistake by going into business with an unsaved man, because an unsaved man is actuated by different principles from those which actuate a saved man. And, of course, it applies to the marriage relationship. What a serious thing it is for a Christian young woman to think of giving her hand in marriage to an unconverted man, in the hope, of course, that some day she will be able to win him for Christ, or what a foolish thing for a Christian man to take an unsaved girl for a life-companion. If they won't come to Christ through your earnest pleading before they are married, you are never likely to win them after the honeymoon is over. They will settle back into their own way, and the chances are that instead of you drawing them your way in the days to come, they will begin to draw you their way. You have heard of the boys who found two linnets in the field. They brought them home and put them in cages hung on either side of their canary. The mother asked the reason for this, and they said, "Well, you see, we got these young, and we have hung them by the side of the canary so that they will be accustomed to listening to the canary sing, and so instead of learning to chirp like a linnet they will learn to sing like the canary." The mother did not say anything, but shook her head, and later on when they came in, they exclaimed, "Why, Mother, listen! Our canary is chirping like a linnet!" That is the way it works. That canary did not get its song back again until they had covered it up for some days, and then when they put it out in the bright sunshine and took the covering off, the little thing began to sing once more. If you are going to count for God you must avoid the unequal yoke. If not, you are going contrary to the Word of God and you cannot expect blessing.

"For what fellowship hath righteousness with unrighteousness?" How can you expect to get on if you have chosen the path of righteousness, and the other, the path of unrighteousness? "What communion hath light with darkness?" Either the darkness must flee before the light, or the light will soon be dimmed by the darkness. You cannot have both at one time. "And what concord hath Christ with Belial?" If you have taken Christ as your Saviour, He is your Lord and your Master, and how can you expect to glorify Him if you link up with one who is a fol- lower of Satan? "Or what part hath he that believeth with an infidel?" By "infidel" it does not mean necessarily an atheist, but it means an unbeliever. You profess to believe in the Lord Jesus, you believe that through His death upon the cross your soul is saved. Well, then, what fellowship can you have with one who refuses to trust your Saviour? Oh, be careful, Christian. You say, "Well, I want to win them for Christ." You will win them best by obedience to the Word of God, not by disobedience. Walk with God yourself in holy separation to Christ, and you can expect your testimony to count with others.

"What agreement hath the temple of God with idols?" The two are in opposition, the one to the other. "For ye are the temple of the living God; as God hath said, I will dwell in them, and walk in them; and I will be their God, and they shall be My people." This is the divine ideal, this is what the Church of God really is, and any company of believers in any given locality is the temple of the living God in that place. How careful we should be then of anything that would mar the temple, of anything that would hinder the display of God among His own people. Do you know that each Christian meeting with any group of believers is either a help or a hindrance to the entire testimony that goes forth from that place? If you are living for God, walking in holy separation to Christ, you are helping the testimony; if walking waywardly, in wilfulness, in worldliness, then you are just helping to that extent to obscure the light that ought to shine forth from the temple of the living God.

The apostle closes that solemn section with this earnest exhortation, "Wherefore come out from among them, and be ye separate, saith the Lord, and touch not the unclean thing: and I will receive you." What does this mean? It means exactly what it says; it does not need any explaining. "Come out from among them" means come out from among them. "Touch not the unclean thing." What does that mean? It means, Touch not the unclean thing. If I tried to explain it, I would only confound and confuse it. Christians are called to walk in separation from the world and to refrain from anything that would contaminate their consciences and hinder their fellowship with God. If you take this position, He says, "I will be a Father unto you, and ye shall be My sons and daughters, saith the Lord Almighty." Is God not my Father if I am a Christian, even though I am not wholly separated from the world? God is the Father of all believers, but He is a Father *unto* us only as we walk in obedience to His Word. I am the father of my child, but if he is wilful and disobedient I cannot be a father unto him in the sense I would like to be, and so God cannot do what His loving heart yearns to do when we are not walking in obedience to His Word.

Let us yield glad, happy obedience to Him, and thus know the blessedness of these words, "I will be a Father unto you, and ye shall be My sons and daughters, saith the Lord Almighty."

LECTURE XIV.

PERFECTING HOLINESS

✓ ✓ ✓

"Having therefore these promises, dearly beloved, let us
cleanse ourselves from all filthiness of the flesh and spirit,
perfecting holiness in the fear of God. Receive us; we have
wronged no man, we have corrupted no man, we have defrauded no man. I speak not this to condemn you: for
I have said before, that ye are in our hearts to die and live
with you. Great is my boldness of speech toward you, great
is my glorying of you: I am filled with comfort, I am exceeding joyful in all our tribulation. For, when we were
come into Macedonia, our flesh had no rest, but we were
troubled on every side; without were fightings, within were
fears. Nevertheless God, that comforteth those that are
cast down, comforted us by the coming of Titus; and not
by his coming only, but by the consolation wherewith he
was comforted in you, when he told us your earnest desire,
your mourning, your fervent mind toward me; so that I
rejoiced the more. For though I made you sorry with a
letter, I do not repent, though I did repent: for I perceive
that the same epistle hath made you sorry, though it were
but for a season. Now I rejoice, not that ye were made
sorry, but that ye sorrowed to repentance: for ye were
made sorry after a godly manner, that ye might receive
damage by us in nothing. For godly sorrow worketh repentance to salvation not to be repented of: but the sorrow
of the world worketh death. For behold this selfsame thing,
that ye sorrowed after a godly sort, what carefulness it
wrought in you, yea, what clearing of yourselves, yea, what

177

indignation, yea, what fear, yea, what vehement desire, yea, what zeal, yea, what revenge! In all things ye have approved yourselves to be clear in this matter. Wherefore, though I wrote unto you, I did it not for his cause that had done the wrong, nor for his cause that suffered wrong, but that our care for you in the sight of God might appear unto you. Therefore we were comforted in your comfort: yea, and exceedingly the more joyed we for the joy of Titus, because his spirit was refreshed by you all. For if I have boasted any thing to him of you, I am not ashamed; but as we spake all things to you in truth, even so our boasting, which I made before Titus, is found a truth. And his inward affection is more abundant toward you, whilst he remembereth the obedience of you all, how with fear and trembling ye received him. I rejoice therefore that I have confidence in you in all things" (2 Cor. 7).

✓ ✓ ✓

I N order properly to understand this chapter we need to remember that some time before the apostle Paul had heard of some very serious wrong-doings tolerated in the Church of God at Corinth. One offence was of greatest gravity; a man had actually entered into an incestuous, adulterous relationship with his own father's wife—his stepmother, of course—and the church, instead of immediately dealing with this great sin and seeking to show the man his wickedness, and if he refused to repent excommunicating him from their fellowship, rather gloried in the breadth that would permit them to tolerate a thing like that and go right on without discipline. There were other offences, brother going to law with brother, etc. When the apostle heard of these things he wanted to visit Corinth, and yet he felt that if he did, it would mean he would have to be very stern in dealing with these questions. He disliked this, and, too, the Spirit of God seemed to hinder his going, so instead of that he wrote them a letter, that letter which we have already taken up, the first epistle to the Corinthians, and in it he pointed out these things and called upon them to act in the fear of God. As to the wicked man, the Word of God was, "Put away from among yourselves that wicked person" (1 Cor. 5: 13).

After having sent the letter Paul was greatly perturbed. The epistle was divinely inspired, and he was a servant of the Lord, but he was a very human personage, just as we are. After he had sent the letter he began to question the wisdom of it; he wondered whether it might simply stir up the flesh in these Corinthians and alienate them further from God and from himself. He questioned whether perhaps it would not have been better if he had gone to them and dealt personally with them, and wondered just what reaction the letter would have upon them. Finally his distress was so keen he could not wait to hear from them in the ordinary way, so he sent his friend and companion, Titus, to Corinth, to find out exactly how they had acted upon receipt of the letter. After waiting some time, still in perturbation of mind (for he loved the Church of God, he loved the saints in spite of their failures and he was fearful lest when he wanted to help he might have hurt, lest when he wanted to bless his message might have had the contrary effect), Titus came and said something like this, "Paul, your letter had the effect you desired it to have. Those brethren in Corinth have taken it as a message from God, and have dealt with this evil thing and have put this man out of their fellowship. He, on his part, has accepted it as divine discipline and is repenting in bitterness of soul. He weeps over his sin and feels utterly unworthy of further recognition of fellowship with the church. They have determined that they are going to keep that assembly clean from all these evils." When Paul heard these things he was greatly rejoiced and sat down and wrote this second letter, and in this chapter he comes to the subject before him.

The first verse properly belongs to the previous chapter: "Having therefore these promises, dearly beloved." That leads us to ask what promises, and so we turn back to chapter six to find out, and we read in the last two verses, "Wherefore come out from among them, and be ye separate, saith the Lord, and touch not the unclean thing; and I will receive you, and will be a Father unto you, and ye shall be My sons and daughters, saith the Lord Almighty." God has given promises of blessing that will accrue to us if we walk in separation from evil, and now we must see to it that we meet the conditions. "Having therefore these promises, dearly beloved, let us cleanse ourselves from all filthiness of the flesh and spirit, perfecting holiness in the fear of God." How do we cleanse ourselves? We cannot cleanse our own consciences from the guilt of sin. God has to do that. Our consciences can be cleansed from sin only by the precious atoning blood of the Lord Jesus Christ. I could not wash out one stain from a guilty conscience. But if a Christian, having been cleansed from my sin by by the blood of Christ, my heart needs daily cleansing, and that is by faith in the Word which God has given. As I receive that Word in faith and I act upon it, I cleanse myself from all filthiness of the flesh and spirit.

What is the difference between filthiness of the flesh and filthiness of the spirit? There are two classes of sin, and all sin is filthy in the sight of God. Filthiness of the flesh refers to sins of the body, and there are so many of them, unholy lusts, unbridled appetites. Drunkenness, gluttony, licentiousness, inordinate affection, are all sins of the flesh, and though at the present time our abominable philosophies throw a glamour over these things they are utterly vile in God's sight. My own heart is stirred to indignation as I pick up the newspapers or magazines of the day, for there is hardly one that does not seem to be glorifying sin. Alluring advertisements suggest that the grandest thing in the world is to indulge in the free use of strong drink. There are beautiful pictures of lovely women drinking with their men friends, and of the whole family gathered around the table being served cocktails. All this in reputable magazines going into Christian homes to teach our children that drinking is a fashionable and decent and respectable thing, when God's Word says, "Woe unto him that giveth his neighbor drink, that puttest thy bottle to him, and makest him drunken also" (Hab. 2: 15). "Look not upon the wine when it is red" (Prov. 23: 31). All men's efforts to make money by causing us to become a nation of drunkards is something for which they will have to account to Almighty God some day. My heart is stirred when I think of these things. You see the same thing in regard to the vile habit of tobacco. Pick up the magazines that come to your home, and you will see some dainty young woman with an abominable cigarette in her fingers. They are trying to teach our girls that if they would be up-to-date they must become cigarette fiends. I cannot understand Christian women tolerating things like that. There is not one good reason why Christian women, or men either, should poison their bodies with tobacco.

And then again take our bookstands. They are filled with the vilest pornographic literature, glorifying fornication and adultery, as though man reaches the highest and noblest in life when he throws the reins upon every low appetite and lives to please himself in absolute indifference to purity and decency and goodness. Christians ought to be very careful to give everything like this a wide berth. "Let us cleanse ourselves from all filthiness of the flesh," let us avoid everything that has to do with the filthiness of the flesh.

What about filthiness of the spirit? Vanity, pride, conceit, haughtiness, and unbelief are just as evil as these other things in the sight of God. Take this dainty girl who stands in front of her mirror trying to make a work of art out of her face in order to attract the attention of the opposite sex, that vanity that is so characteristic of her is as truly filthy in the sight of God as the other sins I have been mentioning. Take that man who is so haughty and proud, and is seeking power and authority over his fellows, constantly looking for admiration on the part of men who like himself are going on to the grave, that haughtiness, that pride, is in God's sight abso-

lutely filthy. "Let us cleanse ourselves from all
filthiness of the flesh and spirit, perfecting holiness in the fear of God." Mark this, none of us
have yet attained to perfect holiness. We are
commanded to "follow peace with all men, and
holiness, without which no man shall see the
Lord" (Heb. 12:14). But we follow that which
is still before us; we have not attained to holiness,
but we are to aim at "perfecting holiness in the
fear of God." As we submit ourselves to the
Word and seek to judge those things that we see
to be contrary to the mind of God, we will grow
in grace and thus become holier men and women
as the days go by.

Beginning with verse 2 and going on to the
end of the chapter, the apostle sets before the
Corinthians the exercises that he had in regard
to them, and the joy that now fills his soul because they are indeed "perfecting holiness in the
fear of God." First, he mentions his claim to
their obedience, for he had no right to be heard
if in himself he was not seeking to live out what
he taught them. But he says, "Receive us; we
have wronged no man, we have corrupted no
man, we have defrauded no man." Many a one
who has taken the position of a servant of Christ,
who is recognized as a minister of the gospel,
has failed terribly because of lack of care right
here. Paul can face the whole world and can

say, "We have wronged no man, we have corrupted no man, we have defrauded no man." He did not teach that which would injure others; he did not by his behavior set a bad example to others; he had no part in turning the grace of God into lasciviousness, as some had done, or in defrauding another. He never had to do with money matters that were shady; he did not collect money for one purpose and use it for another; he did not pretend to be raising funds to do certain things with them and then allow them to be turned aside into some other channel. He was straight in all his dealings, and that is what God expects of every servant of His.

And then he says, as it were, "I am not saying this about myself to condemn you, but I want you to know that I am entitled to be heard because I am living what I preach. I love you too much to want to condemn you; you are my children in the Lord, and I am concerned about you, and I want to help you, not to hinder you. My boldness of speech is great, I have told other people of the wonderful work of grace that has taken place in Corinth, and I was in great distress when you were going wrong, but now I am joyful even though I am passing through tribulation."

"When we were come into Macedonia, our flesh had no rest, but we were troubled on every side; without were fightings, within were fears. Nevertheless God, that comforteth those that are cast down, comforted us by the coming of Titus." What was the comfort Titus brought? "Not by his coming only, but by the consolation wherewith he was comforted in you." It did him good to hear how earnest they were in putting away the evil-doer from their assembly. Titus told Paul of their "earnest desire," and their "mourning." It was not vindictiveness that put him away—they mourned over him. Paul rejoiced in their loyalty to him as the one who had led them to Christ. The previous epistle, he found, did upset them. He was not sorry now that he wrote it, but says, "Now I rejoice, not that ye were made sorry, but that ye sorrowed to repentance...for godly sorrow worketh repentance to salvation not to be repented of." This is the divine principle. Of course he is speaking to them as Christians. They had been saved by acting upon the truth revealed to them. But the same principle always prevails. "Godly sorrow worketh repentance not to be repented of." "Repentance unto salvation"—that leads a man to judge himself in the presence of God, and thus be in the place where God can bless him.

"For behold this selfsame thing, that ye sorrowed after a godly sort, what carefulness it wrought in you, yea, what clearing of yourselves, yea, what indignation, yea, what fear, yea, what

vehement desire, yea, what zeal, yea, what revenge! In all things ye have approved yourselves to be clear in this matter." They were
determined to see that the Church now was clear
of all complicity with evil, they were stirred to
the very depths of their souls. The evil must be
dealt with if blessing would come, and they valued
God's favor above all else.

And so Paul says, "Though I wrote unto you,
I did not do it in order to punish the man that
did the wrong, nor in order to comfort the man
who was wronged." It is impossible, you see, for
any one to commit that sin without doing wrong
himself and wronging others. But he makes it
clear that he wrote to show that he really loved
them and wanted them to be right with God—
that his care for them in the sight of God might
appear unto them. Now because of the way they
had acted his heart was filled with gladness, and
his boasting that he expressed when talking
about them had been fully justified, and Titus'
inward affection was more abundant toward
them, whilst he remembered the obedience of
them all, how with fear and trembling they received him. What a happy outcome this was, and
what a lesson it ought to have for us today! We
are continually praying for revival, but we can
pray for that from now until doomsday and will
not get it, unless as individuals we judge any evil

that is in our own lives. It will never come until we as individuals put away all filthiness of the flesh and spirit. That is what God is waiting for, for His people individually to get right with Him. Mark, it is not for us to look at others and say, "O Lord, Thou knowest what a terrible state Thy people are in. Help them to get right with Thee." No; it is, "Show me any extent to which any sin has found lodgment in my heart and life, and give me grace to judge it in Thy holy presence, that I may put away 'all filthiness of the flesh and spirit, perfecting holiness in the fear of God.' "

A woman came to a servant of Christ and said, "I wish you would go and talk to my husband; he is getting where he never stays home at night; he sets the children such a bad example; and if I talk to him, he slams the door and out he goes."

The minister happened to know something of that home, and said to the woman, "Before we pray for your husband there is something I want to talk to you about. What about that vile temper of yours? Go to God and say, 'O God, I come to Thee confessing my vile, wicked temper; my bad temper is driving my husband from home; it is alienating my children; my bad temper is bringing dishonor on the name of the Lord. Deliver me from that bad temper, that thus I may be able to present the sweetness and graciousness of

Christ, and so help my husband and children.'"

Did she do it? She jumped to her feet and **ran** out in another fit of temper. Let us "perfect holiness in the fear of God" by cleansing *ourselves* from "all filthiness of the flesh and spirit," and then we may expect blessing.

THE GRACE OF LIBERALITY

✦ ✦ ✦

"Moreover, brethren, we do you to wit of the grace of God bestowed on the churches of Macedonia; how that in a great trial of affliction the abundance of their joy and their deep poverty abounded unto the riches of their liberality. For to their power, I bear record, yea, and beyond their power they were willing of themselves; praying us with much intreaty that we would receive the gift, and take upon us the fellowship of the ministering to the saints. And this they did, not as we hoped, but first gave their own selves to the Lord, and unto us by the will of God. Insomuch that we desired Titus, that as he had begun, so he would also finish in you the same grace also. Therefore, as ye abound in every thing, in faith, and utterance, and knowledge, and in all diligence, and in your love to us, see that ye abound in this grace also. I speak not by commandment, but by occasion of the forwardness of others, and to prove the sincerity of your love. For ye know the grace of our Lord Jesus Christ, that, though He was rich, yet for your sakes He became poor, that ye through His poverty might be rich. And herein I give my advice: for this is expedient for you, who have begun before, not only to do, but also to be forward a year ago. Now therefore perform the doing of it; that as there was a readiness to will, so there may be a performance also out of that which ye have. For if there be first a willing mind, it is accepted according to that a man hath, and not according to that he hath not. For I mean not that other men be eased, and ye burdened: but by an equality, that now at this time your abundance may be a supply for their want, that their abundance also may be a supply for your want: that there may be equality: as it is written, He that had gathered much had nothing over; and he that had gathered little had no lack. But thanks be to God, which put the same earnest care into the heart of Titus for you. For indeed he accepted the exhortation; but being more forward, of his own accord he went unto you. And we have sent with him the brother, whose praise is in the gospel throughout all the churches; and not that only, but who was also chosen of the churches to travel with us with this grace, which is administered by us to the glory of the same Lord, and declaration of your ready mind: avoiding this, that no man should blame us in this abundance which is administered by us: providing for honest things, not only in the sight of the Lord, but also in the sight of men. And we have sent with them our brother, whom we have oftentimes proved diligent in many things, but now much more diligent, upon the great confidence which I have in you. Whether any do enquire of Titus, he is my partner and fellow-helper concerning you: or our brethren be enquired of, they are the messengers of the churches, and the glory of Christ. Wherefore show ye to them, and before the churches, the proof of your love, and of our boasting on your behalf" (2 Cor. 8).

✓ ✓ ✓

WE have in this chapter a very wonderful window through which we may look into conditions prevailing in the early Church. We are allowed, nineteen hundred years later, to look through this chapter, as it were, into the very life of God's people so long ago. A famine had taken place in Palestine, and many of the Jewish believers, many of the early Christians in Jerusalem and Judea and other parts of

Palestine, were suffering. There was a real depression prevailing all over that land. Naturally in such a time the world cares for its own. In those days especially there would be very little provision made, very little concern shown, regarding those who had trusted the Lord Jesus Christ. By that very confession of faith in Him they had lost their standing in Judaism and were obnoxious to the idolatrous system of the Roman Empire. But just as soon as word of their plight reaches the apostle laboring in a distant land, he says, "Now here is the opportunity for the Christians among whom I am working to show how true their fellowship is with their brethren over there in Judea," and he immediately stresses the importance of self-denial, of giving generously in order that the needs of the Judean believers may be met.

A chapter like this is most instructive to us, for we are still in the world where believers will be going through difficulties and hardships, and we are to be helpers in this way of one another's faith. We think particularly of those who have left their homes, left the opportunity of making a good salary in this land, to go out to carry the gospel of the grace of God among the heathen. What a shame it would be to us if they were left there suffering for the lack of temporal necessities. It is our privilege to show our fellowship with them by denying ourselves, in order to keep them free from care along these lines. There is a wonderful principle that runs all through this chapter, the principle of brotherly fellowship with those in need. You will notice that the apostle had already brought this matter before the Corinthians when he went through there the year before. He said, "What can you do?" "Well," they had said, "we will give something; we will do our best." Now he has been up in Macedonia laboring, and he is coming back through Corinth on his way to Jerusalem, and so writes and practically says, "I hope you are prepared to keep the pledge you made a year ago."

Sometimes people say, "I do not believe in making pledges." At the bottom of that there may be utter selfishness. We all make pledges. We make a pledge to the landlord when we promise to pay him so much a month. If you are running a bill at the grocery store, you have pledged to pay for what you purchase. You make pledges when you buy anything on the installment plan. Are God and the work of God the only Person and the only thing that are of so little importance that you cannot risk making a pledge in order to help in Christian service? These Corinthians had made a pledge, and the apostle says, in verse 11, "Now therefore perform the doing of it; that as there was a readiness to will, so there may be a performance also out of that which ye have." They had been willing to do this, they had said, "We will do something, Paul, when you come back again." "Now," he says, "you keep that pledge; it may take self-denial; you may have to do without a great many things you want, but these Christians in Judea are doing without very much more." And so we may have to do without some luxuries if we are going to make and keep a proper pledge toward our missionaries, but they are doing without far more. They do not have grand pianos, expensive radios, motor-cars, they do not have beautiful homes and furniture, they are doing without these things for Jesus' sake, and so we can do without many things in order to help them on. Let us look at this a little more carefully.

In the first verse of this chapter he says, "Moreover, brethren, I want you to know of the grace of God bestowed on the churches of Macedonia." How was that grace manifested? Many of us talk a great deal about grace and show very little. God has manifested grace toward us, and how full of grace our lives ought to be. These Macedonians had been saved by grace, and now the rich grace of giving is bestowed upon them. Giving is a grace. "How that in a great trial of affliction the abundance of their joy and their

deep poverty abounded unto the riches of
their liberality." Notice four expressions here:
"Great trial of affliction," "abundance of joy,"
"deep poverty," "riches of liberality." Is it
not remarkable to find all four of these expressions brought into such an intimate relationship? They were going through a great trial, "a
great trial of affliction." But out of "the abundance of their joy," yet coupled with "their deep
poverty," they gave, and it "abounded unto the
riches of their liberality." I do not think that
means that they gave large sums. They probably
did not have large sums to give, but the little was
regarded by God as a larger gift than if very
much more had come from people far more
wealthy than the Macedonians. God's way of
estimating gifts is different from ours. He esti-
mates our gifts, not by the amount we give, but
by the amount we have left. If a man is a mil-
lionaire and gives a thousand dollars, that does
not count as much as one who has an income of
a dollar a day and gives a dime. And so we need
not be afraid to bring our little gifts, thinking
He may despise them. He said of the poor widow,
"She hath cast in more than they all...for she
gave of her poverty all the living that she had"
(Luke 21: 4).

They were taking up a missionary offering once
in a Scotch church. One rather close-fisted

brother was there, known to be worth something like £50,000, which in those days was considered a fortune, and as the deacons went around taking up the offering, one of them whispered to him, "Brother, how much are you going to give?"

"Oh, well; I will put in the widow's mite," he said, and prepared to put in a penny.

"Brethren," the deacon called out, "we have all we need; this brother is giving £50,000."

If he was going to give the widow's mite, he would have to give all he had, you see. It is the widows who give like that, not the rich folk.

But these poor Macedonians out of their poverty gave, and gave with joy. They did not give grudgingly; they were glad to do what they could; and the apostle says, "For to their power, I bear record, yea, and beyond their power they were willing of themselves." They gave to the very limit, and would have given more if they could have done so.

"How much are you going to give, brother?" somebody asked. "Oh," he said, "I guess I can give ten dollars and not feel it."

"Brother," said the first man, "make it twenty, and feel it; the blessing comes when you feel it."

These people gave until they felt it, and they had to pray the apostle to receive their gifts. It would be a great treat to get to the place where that would be the case. It seems that at

Macedonia the apostle just mentioned the need, and then we read, "Praying us with much intreaty that we would receive the gift, and take upon us the fellowship of the ministering to the saints."

In the next verse you can see how they did it. "And this they did, not as we hoped, but first gave their own selves to the Lord, and unto us by the will of God." You see, if I have given myself to the Lord, the rest all follows.

> "Naught that I have my own I call,
>   I hold it for the Giver;
> My heart, my strength, my life, my all,
>   Are His, and His forever."

And so, because they insisted, he says that he has asked Titus to go on to the Corinthians and get their gift, and add it to that of the Macedonians.

"Therefore as ye abound in every thing, in faith, and utterance, and knowledge, and in all diligence, and in your love to us, see that ye abound in this grace also." In other words, you with your fine homes, you with your elegant dress, with all your privileges, you have everything that heart could wish, you who believe that business is business, now see that you abound in this grace also, see that you are just as rich in the grace of giving as in anything else. "I speak not by commandment," I am not commanding you. I am not going to order you to give. This is the dispensation of the grace of God. "I speak not by commandment, but by occasion of the forwardness of others, and to prove the sincerity of your love." In other words, I am trying to make you ashamed as I tell you what others have done, and he points them to the supreme example of self-abnegation. "For ye know the grace of our Lord Jesus Christ, that, though He was rich, yet for your sakes He became poor, that ye through His poverty might be rich." How can I speak of following Him, how can I speak of being saved by His grace, if I do not seek to imitate Him in His self-denying concern for those in need? He saw me in my deep, deep need, and He came all the way from His home in heaven, laying aside the glory that He had with the Father from eternity, down to the depths of Calvary's anguish —and to the darkness of the tomb. He who was rich for my sake became poor, that through His poverty I might be enriched through eternity. And He has left us an example that we should follow His steps.

Notice, Paul never asked for money for himself. Even when he was laboring in Corinth he said, "I robbed other churches...to do you service" (chap. 11: 8). Other churches sent their missionary money to him, but now that they are

Christians he does not want them to forget their responsibilities. He never asks anything for himself, and the true servant of Christ is not going to try to stir people up to do for him, but he will be concerned for the needs of others. Paul would never beg for himself, but he had no shame about pleading most earnestly for others when occasion arose.

"Herein I give my advice: for this is expedient for you, who have begun before, not only to do, but also to be forward a year ago. Now therefore perform the doing of it; that as there was a readiness to will, so there may be a performance also out of that which ye have." And then verse 12, "For if there be first a willing mind, it is accepted according to that a man hath, and not according to that he hath not." It was not a question of saying, "Well, I would do something but am not able," but a question of doing what they could. If you can give only a little to the Lord, give that, and He will multiply it. If you can give a great deal, give it to Him. He looks into the heart. Many a one puts in a dime, and on the books of heaven it goes down as though it were a dollar, but do not put in a dime if you could give the dollar, for that won't go down at all!

"I mean not that other men be eased, and ye burdened: but by an equality, that now at this

time your abundance may be a supply for their
want, that their abundance also may be a supply
for your want: that there may be equality." Some
day things may change; some day it may be the
Corinthians who will be in poverty, and the
Jerusalem saints may be sending to minister to
them in their need, but give as unto the Lord,
because it is written in the Old Testament, and
this refers to the manna, "He that had gathered
much had nothing over; and he that had gathered
little had no lack." You remember it was God
who gave the manna, and He said, Just gather
for your need. A man may have said, "Well, I
am going to gather in while the gathering is good.
Bring out all the pots and pails and the wash-tub,
and I will fill them," and he might have had
enough to last him a month. But the next morning when he went to look at it, he would find that
it had bred worms and was worthless. If he did
not use what he got from day to day it went for
nothing, but if he got just a little it saw him
through. After all, you can only use so much of
this world's goods; use the surplus to the glory
of God and the blessing of a needy world.

In verse 16 to the end of the chapter he shows
the importance of carefully handling funds that
are entrusted to the Church. I think that a great
many otherwise well-meaning servants of Christ
have failed tremendously right along this line.

They gather vast sums of money, making themselves responsible for its use, and no one ever knows whether it has been used in the way promised. The apostle says there should never be anything like that. You must handle the funds in such a way that they can be checked up, and people may know that everything has been used aright. And so the apostle would not touch a penny of it, but said, We will appoint accredited men to look after it, and he appointed two unnamed brethren and his friend, Titus, as a committee to handle all the money, to pay it out and to give an account of everything.

"But thanks be to God, which put the same earnest care into the heart of Titus for you. For indeed he accepted the exhortation; but being more forward, of his own accord he went unto you." Paul had urged Titus to do this work, but he was also anxious to do it of his own accord; he was glad to take up this service. And then we read, "And we have sent with him the brother, whose praise is in the gospel throughout all the churches." This brother's name is not given but they knew him well, for he was chosen by the church. "And not that only, but who was also chosen of the churches to travel with us with this grace, which is administered by us to the glory of the same Lord, and declaration of your ready mind." And why did they do this? "Avoiding

this, that no man should blame us in this abundance which is administered by us." In other
words, he did not want anybody to be able to say,
"Oh, Paul is gathering in a great deal of money.
Who knows what he is doing with it! First thing
we know he will be coming out with some very
expensive equipage that he has bought out of that
money."

"Providing for honest things, not only in the
sight of the Lord, but also in the sight of men."
The Lord knows what we do with the money, but
he says, That is not enough; we want God's people to know also. And then, in addition to Titus
and this brother, Paul had sent another one. The
testimony of two men is true, we read, but it is
written, "In the mouth of two or three witnesses
every word may be established" (Matt. 18:16).
"And we have sent with them our brother, whom
we have oftentimes proved diligent in many
things, but now much more diligent, upon the
great confidence which I have in you." He found
a man who was an expert in business matters,
and says, We have sent him along too.

And then he gives a little word of commendation of these brethren. "Whether any do inquire
of Titus, he is my partner and fellow-helper concerning you: or our brethren be inquired of, they
are the apostles of the churches (the word 'messenger' there is the word 'apostle'), and the glory

of Christ. Wherefore show ye to them, and before the churches, the proof of your love, and of our boasting on your behalf." The proof of love is in giving. We say we are interested in missions—prove it by giving. We say we are interested in poor saints—prove it by giving. We say we are interested in supporting the Lord's work—prove it by giving. God gave—"God so loved the world, that He gave His only begotten Son." Christ so loved the Church that He gave Himself for it, and now we who through grace know God as our Father and Christ as our Saviour are called upon to show our love by giving.

CHRISTIAN GIVING

✔ ✔ ✔

"For as touching the ministering to the saints, it is super-fluous for me to write to you: for I know the forwardness of your mind, for which I boast of you to them of Macedonia, that Achaia was ready a year ago; and your zeal hath provoked many. Yet have I sent the brethren, lest our boasting of you should be in vain in this behalf; that, as I said, ye may be ready: lest haply if they of Macedonia come with me, and find you unprepared, we (that we say not, ye) should be ashamed in this same confident boasting. Therefore I thought it necessary to exhort the brethren, that they would go before unto you, and make up before-hand your bounty, whereof ye had notice before, that the same might be ready, as a matter of bounty, and not as of covetousness. But this I say, He which soweth sparingly shall reap also sparingly; and he which soweth bountifully shall reap also bountifully. Every man according as he purposeth in his heart, so let him give; not grudgingly, or of necessity: for God loveth a cheerful giver. And God is able to make all grace abound toward you; that ye, always having all sufficiency in all things, may abound to every good work: (As it is written, He hath dispersed abroad; he hath given to the poor: his righteousness re-maineth forever. Now He that ministereth seed to the sower both minister bread for your food, and multiply your seed sown, and increase the fruits of your righteousness;) being enriched in everything to all bountifulness, which causeth through us thanksgiving to God. For the administration of this service not only supplieth the want of the saints, but is abundant also by many thanksgivings unto God; whiles by the experiment of this ministration they glorify God for your professed subjection unto the gospel of Christ, and for your liberal distribution unto them, and unto all men; and by their prayer for you, which long after you for the exceeding grace of God in you. Thanks be unto God for His unspeakable gift" (2 Cor. 9).

✐ ✐ ✐

IN this chapter the Spirit of God brings before us in a very impressive manner our responsibility, as believers in our Lord Jesus Christ, to give of our means both for the support of the Lord's work and in order to meet the necessities of Christians who are in distressing circumstances.

It was given to our Lord Jesus to enjoy in a way peculiarly rich and full the happiness of giving. He through whom all things came into being, and for whom they all exist, came into this lower part of His creation, not to be ministered unto but to minister, and to give His life a ransom for many. The apostle Paul, in addressing the Ephesian elders, calls upon them to "remember the words of the Lord Jesus, how He said, It is more blessed to give than to receive" (Acts 20: 35). This naturally raises the question, When, and under what circumstances did He so speak? And at first perhaps one is surprised to find that the four Gospels will be searched in vain to locate any such expression. In other words, the inspired records of the life and sayings of our blessed Lord do not tell us that He used these words on any occasion. And yet the apostle quotes them as though they were well known, as undoubtedly they were, and had frequently been used by the Saviour in the days of His flesh. In fact the tense of the original suggests frequent repetition, and we might render the passage as follows: "Remember the words of the Lord Jesus, how He was wont to say, It is more blessed to give than to receive." That is, it was customary with Him to so speak. He used the words so frequently that His inspired biographers did not even find it necessary to quote them, but wherever His disciples went—those who had known Him on earth —they carried with them this little bit of personal recollection; and so the story went everywhere in the early Church, that it was a frequent thing for the Lord to use the words Paul referred to.

What light this throws upon His character, and how it emphasizes the deep-toned joy He found in imparting good to others. "More blessed" is really "happier;" so that we are justified in reading, "It is happier to give than to receive." He never gave grudgingly. To Him it was a joy to share with those in need. He delighted in communicating the riches of His grace to poverty-stricken, bankrupt souls. Doubtless, often as He fed the multitudes, healed the sick, or ministered in some other way to human need, He would turn to the disciples nearest Him and say quietly and with a sense of deep satisfaction, "It is more blessed to give than to receive."

The Holy Spirit would have us take His example and His words to heart. We are naturally so self-centered that we are inclined to believe the greatest happiness is found in receiving rather than in giving. We all enjoy receiving gifts. We delight in receiving praise, love and adulation. We sometimes imagine that if everything that our hearts crave could be poured out upon us, we would be supremely happy. But this is a total mistake. The happiest people in the world are those who give most unselfishly; and herein lies the challenge to Christians everywhere to whom God has entrusted the means of furthering His interests in the world by financial gifts. Those who go forth for the name's sake of the Lord Jesus, leaving home and loved ones, leaving too all opportunity of earning a livelihood and accumulating wealth, should be in a very special way objects of interest to those who would enjoy the blessedness of which the Lord Jesus speaks. In the Third Epistle of John, we note the commendation of the aged apostle to the Elder Gaius. He writes, "Beloved, thou doest faithfully whatsoever thou doest to the brethren, and to strangers; which have borne witness of thy charity before the church: whom if thou bring forward on their journey after a godly sort, thou shalt do well: because that for His name's sake they went forth, taking nothing of the Gentiles. We therefore ought to receive such, that we might be fellow-helpers to the truth" (3 John 5-8). Undoubtedly the reference was primarily to travelling preachers of the gospel, those whom we call missionaries. Unable to provide for themselves, they were cast entirely upon the Lord, and He on His part met their needs through the gracious gifts of faithful Christians in the home churches, who found real joy in this delightful fellowship.

Shall we not ask ourselves to what extent we have entered into the mind of Christ in regard to this gracious ministry? Are we too experiencing the joy that comes through giving as enabled by God, in order that His servants may be maintained in the path of usefulness in lands far away where they know little of Christian fellowship, but often experience much in the way of testing and hardship? We need never fear that as we open our hearts and purses to them, we ourselves will be permitted to suffer, for we can be certain that God will be no man's debtor.

> "It never was loving that emptied a heart,
> Or giving that emptied a purse."

And we may recall John Bunyan's lines in the immortal allegory:

> "A man there was, though some did count him mad,
>   The more he cast away, the more he had."

For after all, this is but to say in another manner what God Himself has already told us in His own Holy Word, "There is that scattereth, and yet increaseth; and there is that withholdeth more than is meet, but it tendeth to poverty."

With these thoughts in mind, let us notice how earnestly the apostle Paul stresses the importance of this ministry of giving. He says in verses 1, 2: "For as touching the ministering to the saints, it is superfluous for me to write to you: for I know the forwardness of your mind, for which I boast of you to them of Macedonia, that Achaia was ready a year ago; and your zeal hath provoked very many." You see, a year before they had pledged themselves to give for this fund that Paul was raising, and now he is asking them to fulfil the pledges. "Yet I have sent the brethren, lest our boasting of you should be in vain in this behalf; that, as I said, ye may be ready: lest haply if they of Macedonia come with me, and find you unprepared, we (that we say not, ye) should be ashamed in this same confident boasting." You get the point; do you not? He had gone through the churches of Macedonia urging them to have part in this bounty they were raising for the poor saints in Palestine, and he told them that those in Corinth had already pledged themselves to do something generous, but there had been no cash money, and so he was coming through their district on his way to Jerusalem and he did not want them to make him ashamed. He did not wish to urge and beg them to fulfil their promise, but he desired to show the Macedonian brethren how prompt they were to pay. "Therefore," he says, "I thought it necessary to exhort the brethren, that they would go before unto you, and make up beforehand your bounty, whereof ye had notice before, that the same might be ready, as a matter of bounty, and not as of covetousness." That last expression appears to be a little difficult. The word for "covetousness" might just as truly be translated "extortion." He would have the visiting brethren gather up this sum when they reached Corinth, so that it might not seem as if he had to come to them as a tax-collector, trying to force them to give what they had already promised. He wanted it to be glad, joyous giving, the kind that would glorify the Lord.

"He which soweth sparingly shall reap also sparingly; and he which soweth bountifully shall reap also bountifully." And so he uses a common truism to illustrate a great spiritual reality.

Think of a farmer so foolish, as he goes forth to sow his wheat, as to say, "It is too bad to sow so much to an acre; I think I can get a fair crop by sowing less." Such conduct would be absurd. So it is with us. If we want God's blessing on our work, if we want Him to visit us with power and to be generous with us, we must care for the needs of others. There is an old proverb that has been used so long that it is shiny at the knees and frayed at the edges. It is this: "Charity begins at home." People say you must think of home first, and then if you have anything left, give to others or to foreign missions. Giving to missions is not charity. It is not almsgiving when I contribute of my means in order to carry the gospel to a dying world. It is for this purpose God has left us here in this scene. We make a great mistake in talking about home missions and foreign missions. This world is a foreign land to which our blessed Lord came, and from over yonder He sends us forth to go to all nations to carry this gospel to the very ends of the earth. We want to multiply our efforts a thousand-fold by backing up those who go into the regions beyond. Paul, of course, was referring specially to caring for the poor, but the same principle applies to both.

Now notice the state of the heart that God takes into account when it comes to giving. "Every man according as he purposeth in his heart." Someone says he does not believe in making a pledge. What is a pledge? It is the expression of the purpose of your heart. The apostle says, writing by the Spirit of God, "Every man according as he purposeth in his heart, so let him give." Purpose in your heart, then give; "not grudgingly or of necessity, for God loveth a cheerful giver." You say, "Well, I presume they will think it strange if I do not give anything. So I suppose I had better give a little." Do not give so—"Not grudgingly." He does not want one penny from you if you had rather keep it yourself. God does not want your money if you give it grudgingly or of necessity. "Well," you say, "I think I ought to give. I suppose God holds me responsible and I will have to give." No, no; "not of necessity." God gave freely, gladly. And He does not want anything from you unless you also give willingly and gladly; unless you are thankful to be able to give. "For God loveth a cheerful giver." The word in the Greek is *hilaron*, and may be translated "hilarious." God loves a hilarious giver. Not a giver who says, "Dear me, they are always needing money." but one who says, "What is that? Another opportunity to give to missions! Another chance to help the needy! Well, bless the Lord! What can I give? Yes, I think I can double that." That is a hilarious giver, a cheerful giver.

And the Lord will never be your debtor if you give like that. "And God is able to make all grace abound toward you; that ye, always having all sufficiency in all things, may abound to every good work." You see, you take the right attitude toward God and His Word, and He will take a wonderfully benevolent attitude toward you. Then Paul quotes from Psalm 112, "He hath dispersed abroad; he hath given to the poor; his righteousness remaineth forever." In that psalm God is depicting the typically righteous man. One characteristic is, he is interested in other people. He disperses abroad. He gives to the poor. Righteousness, you know, means consistency with the relationship in which we stand. Now, how can we act consistently if we are neglectful of our attitude toward those in distress and toward the servants of Christ?

"Now He that ministereth seed to the sower both minister bread for your food, and multiply your seed sown, and increase the fruits of your righteousness." God knows you need these things and He will look after you. Righteousness and liberality go together. "Being enriched in everything to all bountifulness, which causeth through us thanksgiving to God. For the administration of this service not only supplieth the want of the saints, but is abundant also by many thanksgivings unto God." It begins with God and ends with God. God is able to make all grace abound toward you as you give of your substance to Him. You give to sustain His servants in distant fields. They are blessed and return thanks to God, and that blessing comes back to you. All the rivers run into the sea; the moisture is caught up from the sea into the clouds; the water comes down on the land from the clouds, and the rivers carry it to the sea again, and so there is a never-failing circle of blessing.

"Whiles by the experiment of this ministration they glorify God for your professed subjection unto the gospel of Christ, and for your liberal distribution unto them, and unto all men." Notice, it is "your professed subjection unto the gospel." It is one thing to say we believe the gospel, but if we say we believe it is the only way for sinful men to come to God, surely we will try to get the gospel out to men.

"And by their prayer for you, which long after you for the exceeding grace of God in you. Thanks be unto God for His unspeakable Gift." This Gift is Christ Himself, and He is absolutely beyond all our powers to properly appreciate.

PAUL VINDICATES HIS APOSTLE-SHIP

✓ ✓ ✓

"Now I Paul beseech you by the meekness and gentleness of Christ, who in presence am base among you, but being absent am bold toward you: but I beseech you, that I may not be bold when I am present with that confidence, wherewith I think to be bold against some, which think of us as if we walked according to the flesh. For though we walk in the flesh, we do not war after the flesh: (for the weapons of our warfare are not carnal, but mighty through God to the pulling down of strongholds;) casting down imaginations, and every high thing that exalteth itself against the knowledge of God, and bringing into captivity every thought to the obedience of Christ; and having in a readiness to revenge all disobedience, when your obedience is fulfilled. Do ye look on things after the outward appearance? If any man trust to himself that he is Christ's, let him of himself think this again, that, as he is Christ's, even so are we Christ's. For though I should boast somewhat more of our authority, which the Lord hath given us for edification, and not for your destruction, I should not be ashamed: that I may not seem as if I would terrify you by letters. For his letters, say they, are weighty and powerful; but his bodily presence is weak and his speech contemptible. Let such an one think this, that, such as we are in word by letters when we are absent, such will we be also in deed when we are present. For we dare not make ourselves of the number, or compare ourselves with some that commend themselves: but they measuring themselves by themselves, and comparing themselves among themselves, are not wise. But we will not boast of things without our measure, but ac-

cording to the measure of the rule which God hath distributed to us, a measure to reach even unto you. For we stretch
not ourselves beyond our measure, as though we reached
not unto you: for we are come as far as to you also in
preaching the gospel of Christ: not boasting of things without our measure, that is, of other men's labors; but having
hope, when your faith is increased, that we shall be enlarged by you according to our rule abundantly, to preach
the gospel in the regions beyond you, and not to boast in
another man's line of things made ready to our hand. But
he that glorieth, let him glory in the Lord. For not he that
commendeth himself is approved, but whom the Lord commendeth" (2 Cor. 10).

✓ ✓ ✓

WHAT a very practical portion of the
Word of God this is, and how grateful
we can be for some of the unpleasant
experiences that came to the apostle Paul, because of the lessons that we may glean from his
attitude regarding them. He had ministered, as
we have seen, for a long time in this famous
Greek city. For a year and six months he had
worked and prayed and toiled, laboring with his
own hands to support himself and those associated with him, while he preached publicly and
from house to house, striving to reach lost sinners and bring them to Christ, and once they were
saved, to present every man perfect in Christ
Jesus. He had seen the work grow and develop
in a marvelous way. He had seen men of marked

ability come in among them who could build them
up, and then, as a true missionary, he had left
them and moved on to other fields, that he might
still carry the gospel to those who had not heard
it. And now having been away from them, he
had learned of a preconcerted movement among
certain enemies of the gospel of the grace of God
to try to turn his own converts away from confidence in him as an inspired and duly authorized
apostle, in order that thereby they might weaken
the faith of those converts in the glorious declaration of the grace of God which he had proclaimed. Paul here had to insist very strongly
upon the authority that had been given him. He
had to defend his apostleship, to magnify his
office. And though it was the very last thing he
delighted to do, he had to call attention to the
work that God had wrought through him and
show that he was truly a sent-one of Christ. They
had seen a lowly tentmaker, his hands often be-
grimed with toil. They had seen him put away
his rough garments to get ready for a preaching
service, and go down to the meeting-place to minister Christ after his working hours.

They had seen a common workingman, and
now they used this against him. "Why," they
said, "he is not an apostle, a man who exists in
the lowly way he lives. How ordinary, how com-
monplace, his calling is from day to day! Do you

call *him* an apostle? Do others of the apostles of Jesus Christ have to work as he does, with their own hands?" And so they despised him the more because of his very humility. He replies, "I Paul myself beseech you by the meekness and gentleness of Christ." What did they think of Christ? He was a carpenter and used the saw, the hammer and the adze in the carpenter's shop at Nazareth, and took the lowest place here on earth that He might exalt us to the highest. Well, by His meekness, by His gentleness, I "who in presence am base among you, but being absent am bold toward you, I beseech you, that I may not be bold when I am present with that confidence wherewith I think to be bold against some, which think of us as if we walked according to the flesh." You see, he had to write them a very strong letter in order to point out and reprove serious things that were being done in the church at Corinth. There was party-strife there and, among other things, they were setting one servant of God against another. Some were saying, "I am of Paul, and I of Apollos, and I of Cephas," and others were declaring, "We alone are of Christ." And Paul had to rebuke all that and rebuke it sternly. And then there were brethren going to law one with another, and there were other things that had to be dealt with, and so his letters were sharp and strong.

But now he has to deal with those who are his detractors. They were saying, "It is all right, he can sit down in the privacy of his own study and write boldly, but if he had to meet you face to face, he would not dare to talk like that." And Paul says, as it were, "I hope there will not be any occasion for it. I write you a letter rather than to come to see you, because I do not want to have to say these stern things to you: I love you too tenderly to wish to hurt you. I thought I might help you with my letters, but if you do not respond to them I will have to tell you face to face what I mean, and show that we have divine authority backing up everything we have to say."

"For though we walk in the flesh, we do not war after the flesh." We are in the flesh, it cannot be otherwise, but, he says, we do not war according to the flesh. We are not men who, as servants of Christ, are actuated by mere fleshly motives. "The weapons of our warfare are not carnal." We do not behave in a fleshly way, but our weapons, which are those given us by the Holy Spirit of God, are "mighty through God to the pulling down of strongholds; casting down imaginations, and every high thing that exalteth itself against the knowledge of God, and bringing into captivity every thought to the obedience of Christ." What an ideal that is for the servant

of God! The minister of Christ is not sent to
preach eloquent sermons with beautiful resound-
ing platitudes, but to give men the truth of God;
and the effect of this truth upon the conscience
is intended to bring every thought into subjection
to the obedience of Christ, that all human reasoning may come to an end when God speaks, and
that there may be absolute subjection to His will.
If you are not ready to obey the Word of God,
then I have to be in readiness to revenge every
disobedience, he says.

Next he warns them against looking on the
outward appearance. I judge Paul's physical appearance was not that of a great statesman or a
great leader. The Greeks particularly admired
splendid physique, as we may see from the many
magnificent statues they have left behind. But
Paul was probably a very small man. The name
"Paul" means "little one," and people naturally
received names in those days that intimated what
they were. His outward appearance was weak
and his speech contemptible. It may be there
was a hesitancy in his speech, caused possibly
when he was stoned at Lystra, and perhaps he
could not speak with freedom or fluency. So they
despised him because of physical infirmities. But
that little man, though physically weak, was filled
with the power of the Spirit of God, and through
that power had done wonderful things for Christ,

and so he could say, "If any man trust to himself that he is Christ's, let him of himself think this again, that, as he is Christ's, even so are we Christ's." In other words, "I am not much to look at, but I belong to Christ just as much as the fine-looking teachers with heroic figures. I am His servant, and He uses me in spite of my physical infirmity. It is He Himself who has given me direct authority." "Though I should boast somewhat more of our authority, which the Lord hath given us for edification, and not for your destruction." He would not claim authority in order to avenge himself of them, but his authority was for their blessing. In obedience to Him he had brought them the gospel, and now he desired to build them up in Christ. "For his letters," say they, "are weighty and powerful; but his bodily presence is weak." "Well," he says, "wait until I get there, and see." I think there is a little bit of grim humor here. I think the apostle rather smiled as he wrote the next verse: "Let such an one think this, that, such as we are in word by letters when we are absent, such will we be also in deed when we are present." We dare not compare ourselves with others, saying, "Well, I can do it better than someone else." Paul says, "No, that is not it. It is not a question merely whether I am able to preach better than others or not. We are all Christ's servants." "We dare not make ourselves of the number, or compare ourselves with some that commend themselves; but they measuring themselves by themselves and comparing themselves among themselves, are not intelligent." It is a very foolish thing to compare or contrast ourselves with others. To every man his work. Every servant of God has some special gift. Whitefield said, "Other men may preach the gospel better than I can, but no man can preach a better gospel."

But now the apostle says, "I have had one definite aim and nothing is going to turn me aside from that." "We will not boast of things without our measure, but according to the measure of the rule which God hath distributed to us, a measure to reach even unto you." "Rule" might be translated "canon." Canon law is the law or rule by which churches are governed. Paul seems to say, "This is the canon that God has given me, a measure to reach even unto you, and that is, that we should preach the gospel in the regions beyond." He says, "My rule as a missionary is not to be occupied so much with churches already established, and certainly not to go where other men have labored, and then add my little to it. I do not want to build on another man's foundation. But my business is to preach the gospel where Christ is not named." It is not wrong to build on other men's foundations. I stand here today, and what am I doing? Well, the best I can do is to build on other men's foundations. But Paul recognizes that. He says, "I have laid the foundation and another man buildeth thereon." But he declares, "My rule is not to build on other men's foundations." He was a foundation layer. He went from country to country, from city to city, from village to village, carrying the gospel of the grace of God. He sought to lead souls out of darkness, who had never heard the message of light before. Then he would gather them together by the Spirit's power into little groups. We hear that word "indigenous" used so much these days, referring to missionary work. The natives are encouraged to establish "indigenous churches." This was Paul's mode of operation. He had preached at Corinth, and away he went. Other men could come now and build them up, but he must carry the gospel to the ends of the earth. What a missionary Paul was! He was a pattern foreign missionary for our entire age. There have been many since then who have gone forth in the same spirit that actuated him. This is the business of the Church, and if we cannot all go, we can help those to go who are free to do it, and we can pray and give that they may work on unhindered by want.

We are not, says Paul, "to boast in another

man's line of things made ready to our hand. But
he that glorieth, let him glory in the Lord."
Whether one is building on another man's foundation or seeking to tell men and women in distant
lands of Christ, it is all the same: "He that
glorieth, let him glory in the Lord. For not he
that commendeth himself is approved, but whom
the Lord commendeth." Here, then, is the ideal
missionary as exemplified in the life of the apostle
Paul. May we all in some measure at least enter
into it. How wonderfully Paul sought to follow
his Master. He said, "Follow me, as I follow
Christ." Christ came from the heights of glory
down into the depths of sin and woe, and He trod
the path of humiliation and shame, and at last
went to the cross and there gave His life for the
redemption of guilty men. "He that saith he
abideth in Him ought himself also so to walk,
even as He walked."

Lecture XVIII.

ESPOUSED TO CHRIST

✦ ✦ ✦

"Would to God ye could bear with me a little in my folly: and indeed bear with me. For I am jealous over you with godly jealousy: for I have espoused you to one husband, that I may present you as a chaste virgin to Christ. But I fear, lest by any means, as the serpent beguiled Eve through his subtilty, so your minds should be corrupted from the simplicity that is in Christ. For if he that cometh preacheth another Jesus, whom we have not preached, or if ye receive another spirit, which ye have not received, or another gospel, which ye have not accepted, ye might well bear with him. For I suppose I was not a whit behind the very chiefest apostles. But though I be rude in speech, yet not in knowledge; but we have been thoroughly made manifest among you in all things. Have I committed an offence in abasing myself that ye might be exalted, because I have preached to you the gospel of God freely? I robbed other churches, taking wages of them, to do you service. And when I was present with you, and wanted, I was chargeable to no man: for that which was lacking to me the brethren which came from Macedonia supplied: and in all things I have kept myself from being burdensome unto you, and so will I keep myself. As the truth of Christ is in me, no man shall stop me of this boasting in the regions of Achaia. Wherefore? Because I love you not? God knoweth. But what I do, that I will do, that I may cut off occasion from them which desire occasion; that wherein they glory, they may be found even as we. For such are false apostles, deceitful workers, transforming themselves into the apostles of Christ. And no marvel; for Satan himself is transformed into an angel of light. Therefore it is no great thing if his

ministers also be transformed as the ministers of righteousness; whose end shall be according to their works" (2 Cor.
11: 1-15).

1 1 1

T HERE is nothing to stir the heart to worship like contemplation of the Word of
God. Satan has done his best to rob us of
this treasure, but we can thank God that it has
been preserved to us all down through the ages.
God's Word is like Himself, it is perfect. We
read, "The words of the Lord are pure words: as
silver tried in a furnace of earth, purified seven
times."

Now the special verses I want to re-read are
2 and 3: "I am jealous over you with godly jealousy: for I have espoused you to one husband,
that I may present you as a chaste virgin to
Christ. But I fear, lest by any means, as the
serpent beguiled Eve through his subtilty, so
your minds should be corrupted from the simplicity that is in Christ."

We have often heard the saying, "Eternal vigilance is the price of liberty," and we need to remember that in these days, when there are so
many different forces seeking to destroy our liberty here in America, when Communism is pro-
posing license instead of liberty, and when others
would propose a kind of a dictatorship instead of
liberty, we ought to be very grateful to God for

the privileges we have enjoyed, and as a people
we should be watchful and careful lest our lib-
erties be fritted away. But it is just as true
that eternal vigilance is the price we must pay
for maintaining the truth of God. There are
many evil forces at work seeking to turn the
Christian away from the revelation that God has
given in His Word. We need not be surprised at
this, for it has always been so. Just as soon as
God began to work in any dispensation, Satan,
the adversary, attempted to discredit the truth
divinely revealed. In the former dispensation
the conflict was between the revelation given
through prophets and priests at Sinai and
through God's servants throughout the centuries
on the one hand, and idolatry of all kinds on the
other. All through the Christian dispensation
the conflict has been between a pure, clear, gospel
testimony and the different substitutes that the
adversary of our souls has presented to men, to
turn them away from the simplicity that is in
Christ. The apostle Paul had to meet this. We
have already seen in these Corinthian letters
how his steps were dogged by those who sought
to turn his converts away from the message that
he brought to them of salvation by grace alone,
to something that would obscure the preciousness
of that grace. Now in this chapter Paul is
obliged to stoop to something that is very dis-

tasteful to him, because of the false accusations which were being made to destroy the confidence of the saints in their teacher, in order that they might refuse the teaching. If the devil cannot induce people immediately to give up some line of truth, then he will attack those whom God has sent forth to defend that truth. He tried to make Paul's converts lose confidence in their teacher, in his spirituality, in his understanding of the truth, in order to discredit his ministry. These men who wickedly opposed Paul's work ridiculed him and made the most unkind remarks, even in regard to his personal appearance and ability. They charged that he was not fit to be a leader of God's people, that he was not an apostle of the Lord Jesus Christ because he was not one of the original twelve, that he had not received his commission from Christ because it did not come through the twelve. They put him down as a free lance. They would have the people believe he was actuated by selfish motives, that he was endeavoring to make a gain of those to whom he ministered. He indignantly refuted such charges. He disliked doing this; he did not enjoy having to defend himself. The man of God would be content to simply go on preaching the Word of God and never mention himself, but here it became necessary. The Corinthians were losing confidence in their teacher, and if they lost

confidence in him, they would lose confidence also
in that glorious message which he had been appointed to carry through the world. He speaks
of his defence as foolishness. He would rather
speak of Christ. The reason he gives is, "I am
jealous for you with godly jealousy." There is
a jealousy that is condemnable, the jealousy that
one teacher might have of another. Servants of
Christ become jealous of each other, and those
who help in the Lord's work become jealous of
each other, and Sunday School teachers become
jealous of each other. All such jealousy is opposed to the Holy Spirit of God. But there is a
jealousy that is pure, that is clean, that is right,
and it is the kind of jealousy that God Himself
cherishes. He says, "I the Lord thy God am a
jealous God." What does He mean? What does
Paul mean? He means that he cannot bear to
see his brethren turn from God to false gods because he knows that it is to their eternal ruin if
they do. His jealousy is not because of self-love,
but because of his love for them. What would
you think of a husband who says of his wife,
"I have absolutely no jealousy when she is petted
by another man?" There is a jealousy, you see,
that is right, and a true, upright husband wants
his wife to be faithful to him, as he feels himself responsible to be true and faithful to her.
And so our God desires to see His people true to

Him and walking apart from the fellowship of
the world. "The friendship of the world is enmity
with God." Paul says to these Corinthians, "I
am jealous over you." He did not want to see
them drifting away, turning aside, following
things that could not profit, and he did not want
them to lose the preciousness of their first love.
He wished to see them ever true to Christ. His
was a godly jealousy, a jealousy like the jealousy
of God. "For I have espoused you to one husband." They were, as an assembly of God, like
an engaged maiden. They had been espoused to
one husband, even Christ. The marriage supper
and the Lamb were yonder in the glory and they
were waiting for His return. Christ is the
espoused husband of the Church. He died for us,
and we belong to Him, and our hearts must be
true to Him. Paul did not want to see them become errant and unfaithful. He wished to be
able to say at the judgment-seat of Christ,
"Blessed Master, here are those whom I won
for Thee, and their hearts have been true to Thee,
and now they are here to be eternally united with
Thee in the glory." He was afraid that this
might not be. There were agencies at work seeking to hinder this. So he says, "I am afraid lest
by any means Satan should beguile you through
subtilty." That is how the devil works. Satan
never says, "Good morning, I am the devil! I

2 Corinthians 11: 3, 4   **231**

want to mislead you, I want to seduce you, I want
to turn your heart away from God, I want to ruin
you for time and eternity." No, he comes with
the fairest pretences and promises, and he endeavors to turn the heart away from Christ by
deception. He deceived Eve. He has been deceiving mankind all down through the centuries.
"I fear, lest by any means, as the serpent beguiled Eve through his subtilty, so your minds
should be corrupted from the simplicity that is
in Christ." Do you know this? God's truth is
always manifested right on the very surface of
His Word. Wherever people have to enter into
a long course of argument in order to support a
system which they are trying to foist on the
saints, it is not the truth of God. Anything not
characterized by a holy simplicity is not God's
testimony. And so, young saint, test every teaching by searching the Word, and if you do not
find it plainly revealed in the Book, reject all
unscriptural reasoning, no matter how learned
may be the man who does the reasoning.

And Paul says to these Corinthians, "If these
men really came to bring you something better,
you might well listen to them." They came to
drag them down to a lower level, to turn their
hearts away from Christ and to offer them a sub-
stitute, not one which was greater or better or
more satisfactory than Christ, but a legal system

which could only occupy them with self and
fancied human merit. "For if he that cometh
preacheth another Jesus, whom we have not
preached, or if ye receive another spirit, which
ye have not received, or another gospel which
ye have not accepted, ye might well bear with
him." If one came to you and said, "I have found
one better than Christ, better than Jesus," well,
if he really has, you might well bear with him.
But you will never find anyone better than Jesus.
Jesus is God's last word to sinners and His last
word to saints. I picked up a theological book
the other day in which the writer said, "The
time has come when we need a new investigation
of the problem of Jesus Christ." Why, my dear
friends, Christ is not a problem! Jesus Christ is
the solution of every problem; He is the One
who makes everything plain and everything clear;
the One "in whom dwelleth all the fulness of the
Godhead bodily." Paul says, if one substitutes
anything for Christ, turn a deaf ear to him. He
says, if you receive another spirit, which you
have not received, if anyone can tell you of any
spirit greater, mightier or higher than the Holy
Spirit of God, who dwells in every believer, then
you might well go after him. But you will never
find another, for the Holy Spirit is God Himself
as truly as the Father is God, and the Son is God.
Many spirits are abroad in the world who seek to

impose upon men, but the Spirit of God, who
dwells in the believer, is the Spirit who delights
to glorify the Lord Jesus. Then he adds, "If one
come with any other gospel than that which you
have received, you might bear with him." But
there is only one gospel. That gospel takes on
different phases at different times. It is called
"the gospel of the kingdom" when the emphasis
is put upon the kingly authority of the Lord
Jesus Christ. It is called "the gospel of the grace
of God" when the emphasis is put upon the
sinner's salvation. It is called "the glorious gospel of God," or "the gospel of the glory of God,"
when the emphasis is put upon the place that the
Saviour now occupies. When it is called "the everlasting gospel" we think of that message that
tells us there is One, and One only, through whom
sinners can be reconciled to God, and that is the
Lord Jesus. Writing to the Galatians, the apostle
says, "Though we, or an angel from heaven,
preach any other gospel unto you than that which
we have preached unto you, let him be accursed."
For there is no other gospel of God than the gospel of His Son, telling sinful men of the way
whereby they may be justified before His face.

If, then, men have nothing else to bring, why
should they want to destroy the confidence of
the people in God's truth? This was a stern
message which Paul did not like to deliver, but

he had to explain things because of the mis-
apprehensions and the unkind and untruthful
insinuations that his enemies were instilling into
the hearts and minds of his converts. "I suppose I was not a whit behind the very chiefest
apostles." He is not speaking of natural ability.
What he means is this: When it comes to service,
I suppose that I was not a whit behind any of them.
God had put His seal upon his ministry. He had
led thousands to the Saviour's feet, and yet they
said he was not an apostle because he did not
know Christ when He was here on earth. Paul
received his apostleship directly from heaven. It
was the risen Christ who appeared to him, "delivering him from the people and the Gentiles"
unto whom he was sent. That was Paul's ordina-
tion to the apostleship. These Corinthians were
God's seal upon his work.

"Though I be rude in speech, yet not in knowledge." He frankly admits that he has not the
gift of eloquence. But no one could declare the
truth more plainly than he. "Though I be rude
in speech, yet not in knowledge; but we have
been thoroughly made manifest among you in all
things." They knew what his life was like when
he lived among them. There was one thing concerning which they found fault with him. He
would not take any money from them! That is
the last thing anyone would find fault with in a

minister in these days! But they said that showed
he could not be a real apostle. He had labored in
Corinth for a year-and-a-half and he would not
let them contribute anything for his support.
His enemies said that if he had known that he
was a real apostle he would have allowed them
to support him, but he did not dare, because he
was not sure of his ground. He had to explain.
"Have I committed an offence in abasing myself
that ye might be exalted, because I have preached
to you the gospel freely?" He had entered a
city which was one of the most voluptuous on the
face of the earth. He said, "I will not be dependent on this people for anything." He went
there to preach the gospel, and even after they
professed to be the Lord's he would not let them
support him. He must make them feel that
everything they received from him was God's free
gift, so that there would not be any idea in their
hearts that he was looking for personal gain.
How did he live? Well, he says, "I robbed other
churches, taking wages of them, to do you service." In other churches they put their contribu-
tions together and sent the money down to Corinth and helped to support him, so that he might
carry on his evangelistic work without asking
anything, lest they should misunderstand his
motives. "When I was present with you, and
wanted, I was chargeable to no man: for that

which was lacking to me the brethren which came from Macedonia supplied: and in all things I have kept myself from being burdensome unto you, and so will I keep myself." He made tents to support himself, and when that money was not enough, then the Lord sent it in from brethren from Macedonia, and thus in one way or another he was enabled to be independent of that critical, fault-finding group in Corinth, who might misunderstand his motives if he received their money. It is hard to please some people; you cannot do it. If you talk loudly they do not like it, and if you talk softly they cannot hear. If you preach the gospel, that is too simple, and if you teach the Word it is too deep! And so Paul could not satisfy these people, but he sought to clear himself at any rate of the charge of selfishness in his testimony.

"As the truth of Christ is in me, no man shall stop me of this boasting in the regions of Achaia." He did not always live like this, but there were special reasons why he should do it in Achaia. Why did he do it? Because he did not love them? God knows. I remember some years ago I was out in Oregon, and there was a sterling old Hollander and his fine family of ten sons and one daughter, who attended nearly all the meetings; and this dear man did not have any assurance of salvation. He was doing his

very best to please God. He was trying to keep
the law, and he was hoping to get the testimony
in some way of his election and know he was
saved. I tried to open up the truth of salvation
by grace for all who believe. The old man would
listen, but he thought it was too easy. I was in-
vited to his home for dinner, and afterwards we
sat down over an open Bible, and I tried to show
him that he could be saved in a moment by simply
trusting in the Lord Jesus, but he was so occupied
with hyper-Calvinism that he could not see the
simple truth and rest in Christ his Saviour. After
four hours I was leaving, and just as I was turning away the dear old man—with his long beard
he looked like Paul Krueger—reached in his
pocket and offered me a gift of five dollars. I
said, "Tell me, are you giving that out of love
for Christ, or are you giving it to try to help
buy your salvation?" He looked at me a moment
or two and he said, "I don't love Christ, I wish I
did." I said, "Keep your five dollars. I appreciate your kindness in offering it, but I do not
want you to get the idea that there is anything
meritorious about giving money to a servant of
Christ." They told me afterwards that he went
to his room and cried like a child. Two years
later I came back, and I shall never forget the
night he came up to me and said, "I love the Lord
Jesus; I have trusted Him as my Saviour; I know

I am His. Will you take the five dollars now?"
I took it, and was glad to try to use it for the
Lord Jesus Christ. That was Paul's idea. The
Corinthians had the wrong attitude about money.
Paul did not want their money for himself. "But
what I do, that I will do, that I may cut off
occasion from them which desire occasion; that
wherein they glory, they may be found even as
we. For such are false apostles, deceitful workers, transforming themselves into the apostles of
Christ." I gather from this that these false
teachers were quite eager for financial gain. Paul
took the opposite attitude. Then again, these
false teachers spoke well, they seemed in most
things to be very much like real servants of
Christ. How do you detect them? By the message they bring. If they do not preach the truth
of God they are not Christ's apostles. But they
seem to be nice men; they speak so graciously
and eloquently; they are personally so attractive.
The apostle says, "No marvel; for Satan himself
is transformed into an angel of light." He does
not come to men in the crude way we usually see
him pictured, with horns and a tail and hoofs.
Why, such a devil would not lead anyone astray!
But a devil who comes as an angel of light, with
kindly, soft, tender words and dulcet tones—that
is the kind of devil that deceives people. And so
Paul says, if "Satan himself is transformed into

an angel of light, it is no great thing if his ministers also be transformed as the ministers of righteousness; whose end shall be according to their works." Did you notice that expression, "his ministers?" Does Satan have ministers? Does the devil have ministers? Yes, that is what Paul says. A man may be cultured and refined and ordained to the ministerial office and profess to teach the Word of God, but all the time he may be Satan's appointee. How can we tell Satan's ministers from Christ's ministers? In one simple way, Paul says. There need be no difficulty about it. If they are Satan's they may talk a great deal about human righteousness, but one thing they do not talk about. Satan's ministers have nothing to say about the atoning blood of the Lord Jesus Christ. Christ's ministers are like the bride in the Song of Solomon. The bridegroom says to her, "Thy lips are like a thread of scarlet." The true servant of Christ has lips that speak of the blood of Jesus. He points sinners to that atoning blood through which alone guilty men may be saved. No matter how much one may insist on righteousness, personal, civic, or national, if he fails to present to men salvation through the precious, cleansing blood of the Lord Jesus Christ, he is one of Satan's ministers. For God has no other message for lost men than that which is linked with the work of Calvary's cross.

PAUL'S SUFFERINGS FOR CHRIST

1 1 1

"I say again, Let no man think me a fool; if otherwise, yet as a fool receive me, that I may boast myself a little. That which I speak, I speak it not after the Lord, but as it were foolishly, in this confidence of boasting. Seeing that many glory after the flesh, I will glory also. For ye suffer fools gladly, seeing ye yourselves are wise. For ye suffer, if a man bring you into bondage, if a man devour you, if a man take of you, if a man exalt himself, if a man smite you on the face. I speak as concerning reproach, as though we had been weak. Howbeit whereinsoever any is bold (I speak foolishly), I am bold also. Are they Hebrews? so am I. Are they Israelites? so am I. Are they the seed of Abraham? so am I. Are they ministers of Christ? (I speak as a fool) I am more; in labors more abundant, in stripes above measure, in prisons more frequent, in deaths oft. Of the Jews five times received I forty stripes save one. Thrice was I beaten with rods, once was I stoned, thrice I suffered shipwreck, a night and a day I have been in the deep; in journeyings often, in perils of waters, in perils of robbers, in perils by mine own countrymen, in perils by the heathen, in perils in the city, in perils in the wilderness, in perils in the sea, in perils among false brethren; in weariness and painfulness, in watchings often, in hunger and thirst, in fastings often, in cold and nakedness. Beside those things that are without, that which cometh upon me daily, the care of all the churches. Who is weak, and I am not weak? who is offended, and I burn not? If I must needs glory, I will glory of the things which concern mine infirmities. The God and Father of our Lord Jesus Christ, which is blessed for evermore, knoweth that I lie not. In Damascus the governor under Aretas the king kept the city of the Damascenes with a garrison, desirous to apprehend me: and through a window in a basket was I let down by the wall, and escaped his hands" (2 Cor. 11: 16-33).

✓ ✓ ✓

I CONFESS to you that when I read words like these, I cannot get away from the thought that in all the nearly fifty years that I have known Christ as my Saviour, and during almost all that time I have been trying to preach His Word, I have just been playing at Christianity. When I think what this dear servant of God of the first century went through for Christ, motivated by a consuming love for the Saviour, I feel that I have a great deal to learn of what it means to be a true minister of the Lord Jesus.

We have already noticed in the study of this letter that there were those who were very jealous of the ministry of the apostle Paul. They would have crowded him out of the various churches had it been possible, they even ignored him in order to prejudice those who had gladly received him as the servant of the Lord. On some occasions, while not exactly stooping to evil-speaking, they had endeavored to insinuate that he had no true ground for counting himself an apostle of Jesus Christ, that after all he was merely an ecclesiastical free lance and that his words should not be accepted, as those of the original twelve apostles, as really inspired of God. It was because of all this, because his own converts were being distressed and upset by such things, that he found it necessary to direct attention to the marks of his apostleship. He seeks to show that God Himself has put His stamp on his ministry by permitting him to suffer for Christ's sake.

Notice first his boasting. He says in verses 16 to 21: "Let no man think me a fool." That is, there were those who would imply that he was simply imagining that he had had a divine commission, that he was just a simpleton and did not know the difference between an idle dream and a heavenly vision, between the direct call of God and the moving of his own human spirit. "Let no man think me a fool"—I am not as simple as that; and yet he is saying, If you do, well, then receive me on that ground, and give me a chance to indulge in a little bit of foolishness in talking about myself. He was altogether at home when speaking of Christ, but when he had to speak of himself, it was most distasteful, and he considered it as mere foolishness. Yet it seemed necessary, in order to clear up this particular difficulty. "That which I speak, I speak it not after the Lord" (he was not speaking as though by direct command of God but foolishly, as it were,) "in

this confidence of boasting." Others had come to
these Corinthians who boasted of their lineage
and of their graces and abilities and gifts, and
Paul says, "Since you like to hear that kind of
thing, I will give you a little of it." "Ye suffer
fools gladly." In other words, the man who
spends time talking about himself is a fool; you
have had some of that, and you seemed to enjoy
it, and so I am going to give you a little more of
it. "Seeing ye yourselves are wise." That was a
bit of irony. You Corinthians are so remarkably
wise that you can let some of the rest of us in•
dulge ourselves. "For ye suffer, if a man bring
you into bondage, if a man devour you, if a man
take of you, if a man exalt himself, if a man
smite you on the face." Paul says, if you can
stand that, you can stand it if I tell you a little
of my personal experiences and of the Lord's
dealings with me.

"I speak as concerning reproach, as though we
had been weak. Howbeit whereinsoever any is
bold, (I speak foolishly,) I am bold also." There
were those who had a great deal to say about
their credentials. He too had something to say
along that line, and so he went on to tell them
something about his lineage. Those who came
troubling them were as a rule Jews who had made
a profession of Christianity, but had never broken
with the old system and come out into the full

place of the new covenant. They boasted of the fact that they were real Hebrews of Abraham's seed, and Paul asks what have they to boast of over himself? "Are they Hebrews? so am I. Are they the seed of Abraham? so am I." I wonder whether this message is going into the homes of any Jewish families. I am quoting the words of an eminent Hebrew Christian of 1900 years ago, one of the most highly educated Rabbis of his day, a man brought up at the feet of the Rabbi Gamaliel, noted for his sanity and sound orthodoxy. This man, Paul, once called Saul of Tarsus, was of all the Jews of his day the man who had the most bitter hatred against Christianity; but something happened to him that made him the outstanding apostle of the new doctrine of the grace of God, and he is telling us something here of what he endured for the sake of the Lord Jesus Christ. Sometimes people say that certain persons change their religion for temporal benefit. It was not a question of changing religion for Paul, but of getting to know the living Christ. And it was not for temporal benefit, for had he remained as he was he would have lived and died as one of the most honored Hebrews of his time. He knew when he confessed Christ Jesus as his Saviour that he would be put out of the synagogue, that his own friends would disown him, look upon him as though dead, and yet he decided to endure it all for Christ's sake. He says, "What things were gain to me, those I counted loss for Christ" (Phil. 3: 7). This man was genuine. Something had taken place in his inner life that made him step right out from Judaism and commit himself to the Lord Jesus Christ as his Saviour.

"Are they ministers of Christ? (I speak as a fool) I am more." Do others boast that they are ministers of Christ? I too am a minister of Christ, and my ministry has been a wider one than theirs. He is not saying, "I am a greater minister, a greater teacher, a greater preacher." What he is saying is this, "I have labored more abundantly than all the rest of them." He had gone from city to city, from country to country, and from continent to continent, giving the glad, glorious message of the grace of God. None of them had excelled him in this or had come near him in time spent and places visited and multitudes preached to. Then he tells how he has suffered for his ministry: "In stripes above measure, in prisons more frequent, in deaths oft." When you turn to the Book of Acts you read once of his being beaten with stripes, but he says, "In stripes above measure." Just once you read of his being in prison, but he says, "In prisons more frequent." We do not get the entire record in Acts. "In deaths oft." He passed through experiences again and again that were harder to bear than dying for Christ would have been.

Then notice the pathos of this, "Of the Jews five times received I forty stripes save one." That was the discipline of the Jewish synagogue. He could have been free of that. When they summoned him for trial on these five occasions, it was by the elders of the synagogue who charged him with teaching things contrary to the law of Moses, and they condemned him to be beaten with forty stripes save one. That was the Jewish way of disciplining those who were adjudged guilty of violation of the law. They were afraid that they might exceed the legal requirements, for God had said that they were not to be unmerciful, and so they gave thirteen stripes on one side, thirteen on the other, and thirteen down the middle of the back. That was the way they beat one who had broken the law of Moses. If Paul had said, You have no authority over me; I am a Christian, and you cannot judge me and pronounce sentence upon me; I will appeal to Rome, he could have been free from all this. He did this when Cæsar's own officers would have violated the law, but when his own brethren, the Jews, pronounced judgment against him, he bowed his head and took it because of his love for them.

He said, "I became a Jew, that I might gain

the Jews" (1 Cor. 9:20). If you want to see how much Paul loved the Jews, you can do so there as you see him tied to that post, with his back bare. Notice his quivering flesh as the thongs come down upon him. And he could have been delivered from it all if he had simply said, "I am no longer a Jew; I am a Christian." But although he was a Christian he could not forget that by birth he was a Jew, and he loved his people. We hear him say on another occasion, "Brethren, my heart's desire and prayer to God for Israel is, that they might be saved" (Rom. 10:1). And so he even bore the synagogue's discipline in order that he might not be alienated from the people he loved and served and suffered for, "that they might be saved."

Then he goes on to tell of what he endured from the Gentiles. "Thrice was I beaten with rods." That was the Roman punishment. "Once was I stoned;" that was at Lystra. "Thrice I suffered shipwreck." You read of his being shipwrecked once in the book of Acts, but there were two more such experiences. "A night and a day I have been in the deep." I suppose the vessel had gone to pieces, and he was floating about clinging to a spar. No one was near, but he was looking to God, and in some way deliverance came. All these things failed to quench that burning ardor that sent him through the world for a generation proclaiming salvation through the Lord Jesus Christ.

Then there were other perils that he suffered. They were eightfold as given in verse 26. "In perils of robbers," that was a very real peril in those days when robbers beset every mountain path, and Paul traveled from city to city mostly on foot. "In perils by mine own countrymen, in perils by the heathen." The Jews hated him, and the Gentile world failed to appreciate the fact that he was God's ambassador to them. "In perils in the city," among the cultured and refined as well as among the uncouth and the ignorant. "In perils in the wilderness, in perils in the sea, in perils among false brethren." This last is perhaps the saddest of all. Those professing the name of Christ and yet untrue to him, those taking the ground of being servants of God and yet showing themselves false brethren, who would have destroyed his good name if they could.

And then he continues, "In weariness and painfulness, in watchings often, in hunger and thirst, in fasting often, in cold and nakedness." Whatever have you and I known of suffering anywhere near like this? We have sung sometimes, but I wonder whether we really mean it:

> "Jesus, I my cross have taken,
>   All to leave and follow Thee;
> Naked, poor, despised, forsaken,
>   Thou, from hence, my all shall be;

Perish ev'ry fond ambition,
   All I've sought, and hoped, and known;
Yet how rich is my condition,
   God and heav'n are still my own."

Do we really mean it when we sing such a song as this? Are we prepared thus to suffer and endure for Christ's sake? This is first-century Christianity, this is what it cost to be true to God in those early days, and yet how faithful God's servants were that we might have this wondrous heritage of the truth today.

But there was another thing that weighed upon him, and only one having the oversight in the Church of God could know the meaning of this: "Beside those things that are without, that which cometh upon me daily, the care of all the churches." Paul carried the people of God upon his heart. He could not go into a place and labor for a while and then be through with them. They were still on his heart, and if they got into trouble, into difficulty, into dissension, it burdened him, and he took it to God and wrote letters to them and tried to help and bless. And now he says, "Who is weak, and I am not weak? Who is offended, and I burn not?" That is, if some one who should know better stumbles one of the weakest, it fills me with indignation. So truly was he a father in Christ to the people of God. And he adds, "If I must needs glory, I will glory of the things which concern mine infirmities." If I must boast, I will not boast in what I have done or what I am, but "I will glory of the things which concern mine infirmities." Just a poor, weak, earthen vessel, and yet God has taken him up and used him to give the message of His glory to a needy world. He could boast in this, that in spite of all his weakness God had seen fit to speak in and through him.

His conclusion is very striking. You might have expected him to tell of some very remarkable experience he had had, in which God showed that, after all, it was His delight to put honor on the man who had stooped so low for the sake of Jesus, but he tells of something that most of us would have left out. "The God and Father of our Lord Jesus Christ, which is blessed for evermore, knoweth that I lie not. In Damascus the governor under Aretas the king kept the city of the Damascenes with a garrison, desirous to apprehend me: and through a window in a basket was I let down by the wall, and escaped his hands." What a picture! And then think of the dignity of some of us. Just imagine him curled up in a basket and dropped over a wall! That is the last view we have of Paul in this chapter. Some one passing might have looked up and said, "Well, dear me, is that the Rev. Dr. Paul?" No, it is Paul, a servant of Jesus Christ, who counted all things but loss for that excellent name, and is ready to be put to shame, is ready to suffer, is ready to endure, in order that Christ may be manifested in him whether by life or by death.

May God teach us who love the same Saviour to emulate this His servant in devotedness to Christ, in glorying in infirmities. Surely our Saviour deserves our best and most devoted service.

> "Alas, and did my Saviour bleed?
> And did my Sovereign die?
> Would He devote that sacred head
> For such a worm as I?"

PAUL'S THORN IN THE FLESH

✔ ✔ ✔

"It is not expedient for me doubtless to glory. I will come to visions and revelations of the Lord. I knew a man in Christ above fourteen years ago, (whether in the body, I cannot tell; or whether out of the body, I cannot tell: God knoweth;) such an one caught up to the third heaven. And I knew such a man, (whether in the body, or out of the body, I cannot tell: God knoweth;) how that he was caught up into paradise, and heard unspeakable words, which it is not lawful for a man to utter. Of such an one will I glory: yet of myself I will not glory, but in mine infirmities. For though I would desire to glory, I shall not be a fool; for I will say the truth: but now I forbear, lest any man should think of me above that which he seeth me to be, or that he heareth of me. And lest I should be exalted above measure through the abundance of the revelations, there was given to me a thorn in the flesh, the messenger of Satan to buffet me, lest I should be exalted above measure. For this thing I besought the Lord thrice, that it might depart from me. And He said unto me, My grace is sufficient for thee: for My strength is made perfect in weakness. Most gladly therefore will I rather glory in my infirmities, that the power of Christ may rest upon me. Therefore I take pleasure in infirmities, in reproaches, in necessities, in persecutions, in distresses for Christ's sake: for when I am weak, then am I strong" (2 Cor. 12:1-10).

✔ ✔ ✔

WE have been occupied with some of the experiences that the apostle Paul went through as he suffered for Christ's sake. You remember we are told, "All that will live

godly in Christ Jesus shall suffer persecution"
(2 Tim. 3: 12). So, if we are not suffering persecution for the name of Christ, the inference is
that we are not living godly. We may be behaving ourselves decently, we may be living respect-
ably, but God does not have the supreme place in
our lives if we do not know something of persecution on the part of a world that hates God and
that nailed His own blessed Son to the bitter
cross.

Paul had identified himself with that cross
from the moment of his conversion. He said,
"God forbid that I should glory, save in the cross
of our Lord Jesus Christ, by whom the world is
crucified unto me, and I unto the world" (Gal.
6: 14). Naturally, the world hated the man that
spurned it. Walk with the world and the world
loves its own. Jesus said, "The world cannot
hate you; but Me it hateth, because I testify of it,
that the works thereof are evil" (John 7: 7).
And so the apostle lived and toiled and suffered
for an entire generation for the name's sake of
the Lord Jesus Christ. But it was not all suffering. There were times of ecstatic joy, there were
moments of wonderful blessing and spiritual re-
freshment. Did others boast of religious experiences? Well, Paul says, if it is the fashion
to boast, I suppose I can boast too. I do not want
to boast of myself, but I can tell you, if you want

to know, something of the great privileges that at times have come to me.

"It is not expedient for me doubtless to glory. I will come to visions and revelations (or manifestations) of the Lord. I knew a man in Christ." He is referring, of course, to himself, but what a wonderful thing to be able to speak as "a man in Christ." Do you know "a man in Christ," in that sense? You remember on one occasion, writing to the Romans, the apostle speaks of some of his own kinsmen, and uses that expression, "Who also were in Christ before me." You see, people are not in Christ by natural birth. You are not in Christ because your father was in Christ before you were born. You are not in Christ because you have had a praying mother. You yourself have to be born of God. Unless regenerated you are not in Christ up to this present moment. "That which is born of the flesh is flesh" (John 3: 6). It may be very attractive flesh, it may be very agreeable flesh, it may even be religious flesh, but it is flesh still. "That which is born of the flesh is flesh; and that which is born of the Spirit is spirit." It is the man who is born of the Spirit who is in Christ, and so Paul says. I have told you something of the hardships I have endured for Jesus' sake, now I want to tell you something of a great experience that came to me once as a man in Christ.

"I knew a man in Christ above fourteen years ago." That is very interesting. This man had had a remarkable experience, and as far as we can learn he had kept it a secret between himself and God for over fourteen years. This is very unlike us. I have an idea, knowing myself as well as I do, that if I had been in the third heaven yesterday, I should be telling you about it this morning. I would forget everything else and tell you what a wonderful time I had in the third heaven, and then if you believed me, you would look at me and say, "What a saint he must be that God should want his company in the third heaven!" and I would be getting glory to myself through telling about this. That is probably the reason Paul kept it a secret; he did not want people to think of him. He did not mind telling of the hard things; he did not mind speaking of the time when he was ignominiously let down over a wall in a basket. That was something that people would sneer at, laugh at, but such a wonderful experience as being caught up into the third heaven he could keep to himself until the proper time. But if others are boasting of experiences, he will tell them of his own. I do not know what attention you may have given to the chronology in connection with the apostle Paul's life. A little over fourteen years before he wrote this second letter to the Corinthians he was laboring in Galatia. He visited the cities of Iconium, Derbe, and Lystra, and the people were so carried away by him that at one time they wanted to worship him as a god, but later persecution broke out, and they turned on him and actually sought to stone him to death. In fact, the moment came when his crushed and bruised body fell in the highway, and as far as anybody could see he was dead, and they dragged him out of the city and threw that body to one side as a bit of worthless refuse. That was apparently the end of the apostle Paul so far as his ministry was concerned. But after his persecutors had gone back into the city, a little group of heartbroken disciples gathered about that body, and one can imagine how desolate they felt. Their father in Christ, the one who had led them to know Christ, who had cared for them in the things of God, lay before them evidently dead, and they were about to make arrangements for a decent burial, when suddenly Paul rose up and gladdened their hearts by what must have seemed like a veritable resurrection. He was ready to go back to the business of preaching the gospel.

What happened to him at that time when his body lay there in a coma? I like to think that it was then he had the experience he refers to here. "I knew a man in Christ above fourteen years ago." That was just about the time they

tried to stone him to death, and God at that time
may have said, "Paul, I am going to give you a
little vacation; I am going to take you up to let
you see the land to which you are going. Come
up with Me, Paul," and he found himself, he says,
"caught up into the third heaven," and he tells
us he was so enraptured by the glories that he
witnessed that he was not conscious whether or
not he was in the body. Observe, it is possible to
be thoroughly conscious, and yet be out of the
body. The body is not the real man. I am not
the house in which I live. I live in this house, but
some day I am going to put off this my tabernacle;
I am going to move out unless it should please
God that I live in the flesh till Jesus returns again.
But if death takes me, the real man leaves the
body. The body dies, but the believer is "absent
from the body, present with the Lord." Paul had
no consciousness of having a body, or on the
other hand, he did not miss his body. "Whether
in the body, I cannot tell; or whether out of the
body, I cannot tell: God knoweth." That always
helps me when I think of my loved ones gone over
to the other side. They have left this scene of
trial and toil and care, and have gone Home to be
forever with the Lord, but they are just as real,
and just as truly intelligent beings out of the
body and with Christ, as they were when they
were down here in the body. In Ephesians 3: 15

Paul speaks of "the whole family in heaven and earth." Paul was not a materialist, he was not a "soul-sleeper," for if he had been, he would have said, "The whole family in the grave and on earth," but he did not recognize any of the family as lying in the grave, it was just their bodies that were there, but the members of the family are in heaven and on earth.

> "Millions have reached that blissful shore,
>   Their trials and their labor o'er,
>   And yet there is room for millions more."

Are you on the way? Have you trusted that blessed Saviour? These all died in faith, they are at Home with Christ which is far better. Do you know Christ? You have often said that you hoped when life was over that you would find a place in heaven. Are you quite sure you would be comfortable there? Are you quite sure you would be happy in heaven? I know people who cannot enjoy an hour at a prayer-meeting who imagine they would enjoy eternity in heaven. If you have not a new nature, a life that is hid with Christ in God, so that you can enjoy Him now and delight in fellowship with His people, how do you expect to enjoy God and fellowship with the saints in heaven? I am afraid that if some of you were suddenly caught up into heaven without any inward change, you would hardly be there before you would be seeking to get out of that holy place because you have not a nature that is in touch with heaven. You do not appreciate the things of heaven now; how could you expect to enjoy them if you went there as you are? "Ye must be born again" (John 3:7), Jesus said. Paul was born again, he had a new life, and when he found himself in heaven he was at home there. If you were suddenly to be called away from the body, would you be going Home?

A dear fellow was dying. He had been brought up in a Christian home, but he had spurned the grace of God, and someone was trying to comfort him, and leaning over him, said, "It won't be long now, and after all, death is only going Home."

He looked up startled and said, "Going Home! What do you mean? This is the only home I have ever known. Death for me will be going away from home, and going I do not know where."

What would it mean to you? Can you sing:

> "My heavenly home is bright and fair,
> No pain nor death shall enter there;
> Its glittering light the sun outshines,
> Those heavenly mansions shall be mine.
> I am going Home to die no more."

Or would death for you mean going away from home? Is this world your home, and would you be going away into the darkness and distance?

Byron says, and Byron was not a Christian, "There are wanderers over the sea of eternity whose bark glides on and on and anchored ne'er shall be." Oh, can you say:

"By faith in a glorified Christ on the throne,
I give up the joys of this world to its own;
As a stranger and pilgrim I plainly declare,
'My Home is up yonder.' But will you be there?"

"Home, Home, sweet, sweet Home,
There's no friend like Jesus,
There's no place like Home."

Paul went Home for a while. He tells us in the next verse, "I knew such a man (whether in the body, or out of the body, I cannot tell: God knoweth;) how that he was caught up into paradise." That word is found three times in the New Testament, and is not a Greek word although written in Greek letters. "Paradise" is a Persian word, and means "a royal garden." It was the name of the garden of the King where every lovely fruit and flower could be found, and it helps me to understand what it is like up yonder. I am glad God has given us flowers, I am glad He has given us fruit. He could have given us shade without fruit, but "He giveth us richly all things to enjoy," and I try never to partake of the fruit of His bounty or to gaze upon the flowers

of His love without being reminded of Paradise.
It is intended to give us a little idea of what it is
like up yonder. When we talk about the believer
not loving the world, we do not mean that he
should not be interested in this creation. He
should love the things that God his Father has
made.

> "Heaven above is softer blue,
>   Earth beneath is sweeter green,
> Something lives in every hue
>   Christless eyes have never seen.
>
> Birds with sweeter songs o'erflow,
>   Flowers with newer beauty shine,
> Since I know as now I know,
>   I am His and He is mine."

And heaven is a place of wondrous beauty.

Paul found himself in a royal garden, and says
he heard "unspeakable words." That really means
words that could not possibly be declared, words
that no human tongue could make plain, the song
of the redeemed, the praises of the saints, the joy
of the angels. Now he says, "Of such an one
will I glory," of this man in Christ he will glory,
but not of himself as a poor lost sinner. "Of
myself I will not glory, but in mine infirmities."
But why? He says, "I will tell you how I got them;
my infirmities were a love gift from my Father."
I once heard of a man who was very wealthy
and lived in a lovely and magnificent manor house.

He had grown up away from God, and then was struck with that dread malady, paralysis, and for many years he had to be wheeled about in a chair, and as a result of that affliction, unable to get out and enjoy the things of the world, his heart turned to the things of God and he found Christ. They used to wheel him down to the gathering of the saints, and trying to half raise himself in that chair he would praise God and say, "O God, I praise Thee for my dear paralysis." He knew that if God had not permitted that infirmity to come upon him, he might have lived and died in independence of God.

And then Paul says, "And lest I should be exalted above measure through the abundance of the revelations, there was given to me a thorn in the flesh, the messenger of Satan to buffet me, lest I should be exalted above measure." You see, there is no danger to any one in the third heaven, but the danger comes if you have been in the third heaven and return to earth. Think of walking up and down the street saying to yourself: "I am the only man in this city who has ever been in the third heaven and come back again." Paul had been there and when he returned God said, "I must not let My servant be spoiled by this experience," and so gave him, we are told, a thorn in the flesh, but He gave it through the devil. Do you know that Satan cannot do one thing against the child of God until the Lord gives him permission? That is the lesson of the book of Job. "Shall we receive good at the hand of God, and shall we not receive evil?" (Job 2: 10). Job took everything from God, and so Paul says that this was given to him lest he be exalted above measure. "For this thing I besought the Lord thrice, that it might depart from me." What was the thorn in the flesh? I cannot tell you because I do not know. Paul has not told us, and there is no use in our guessing about it; but I know it was in the flesh and therefore a physical infirmity. It was a weakness of some kind that pained and hurt just as though one were driving a thorn into the body, it may have been something that affected his public utterances, something humiliating, and he went to the Lord and prayed in agony of soul three times, "O Lord, deliver me from this thing." The Lord finally said, "No, Paul; I am not going to deliver you from it, but I am going to do better than that; I am going to give you grace to bear it." Oh, those unanswered prayers of our lives, how they bewilder some of us! Think of the many unanswered prayers recorded in the Bible.

Abraham prayed, "O God, that Ishmael may live before Thee." Now Abraham meant, "Let him be the inheritor of the promises." But God said, "No; in Isaac shall thy seed be called." How thankful Abraham is today that his prayer was not answered. Moses prayed, "O God, let me go into the land," and God said, "Do not talk to Me about that any more; you cannot go in," and to-day as Moses stands yonder in the glory how glad he is that God had His way. David prayed for the child of Bath-sheba, "Heal the child, and let him live." But God said, "No; I won't heal him; I am going to take him Home," and David bowed his head at last and said, "He cannot come back to me, but I will go to him," and David's heart was drawn toward Heaven in a way it would never have been otherwise, and how thankful he is today that God did not answer his prayer. Elijah went out into the wilderness when an angry woman frightened him. The man who could stand before King Ahab ran away to the juniper tree when Jezebel was after him, and he flung himself down before God and said, "I am no better than my fathers." Did you think you were, Elijah? He found out that he was not, and then he said, "Let me die." How thankful he is today that God did not answer that prayer. Elijah is the only man between the flood and the cross of Christ who never died at all. He went to heaven without dying. And Paul prayed, "Remove the thorn from my flesh," and the Lord said, "I won't remove it, but I will give you grace to bear it." Have you a thorn, some great trial, some infirmity, some distress, something that is just burdening your heart and it seems as though you will break under it? You have prayed and prayed, "O Lord, deliver me from this." It may not be the will of God to deliver you, but He says, "My grace is sufficient for thee: for My strength is made perfect in weakness." When Paul heard that, he said, "Most gladly therefore will I rather glory in my infirmities, that the power of Christ may rest upon me." The weaker I am the better opportunity Christ has to manifest Himself in me.

And then in the concluding verse of this section he says, "Therefore I take pleasure in infirmities, in reproaches, in necessities, in persecutions, in distresses for Christ's sake: for when I am weak, then am I strong." May God give each one of us to take that place of subjection to the will of God where we can glory in infirmities.

HELPING OR HINDERING CHRISTIAN TESTIMONY

✓ ✓ ✓

"I am become a fool in glorying; ye have compelled me: for I ought to have been commended of you: for in nothing am I behind the very chiefest apostles, though I be nothing. Truly the signs of an apostle were wrought among you in all patience, in signs, and wonders, and mighty deeds. For what is it wherein ye were inferior to other churches, except it be that I myself was not burdensome to you? Forgive me this wrong. Behold, the third time I am ready to come to you; and I will not be burdensome to you: for I seek not yours, but you: for the children ought not to lay up for the parents, but the parents for the children. And I will very gladly spend and be spent for you; though the more abundantly I love you, the less I be loved. But be it so, I did not burden you: nevertheless, being crafty, I caught you with guile. Did I make a gain of you by any of them whom I sent unto you? I desired Titus, and with him I sent a brother. Did Titus make a gain of you? walked we not in the same spirit? walked we not in the same steps? Again, think ye that we excuse ourselves unto you? we speak before God in Christ: but we do all things, dearly beloved, for your edifying. For I fear, lest, when I come, I shall not find you such as I would, and that I shall be found unto you such as ye would not: lest there be debates, envyings, wraths, strifes, backbitings, whisperings, swellings, tumults: and lest, when I come again, my God will humble me among you, and that I shall bewail many which have sinned already, and have not repented of the uncleanness and fornication and lasciviousness which they have committed" (2 Cor. 12: 11-21).

THE Church of God is the holiest thing there is on earth, and yet there are a great many imperfections in that Church. It is absolutely the best thing in the world today. If you were suddenly to take the Church of God out of this world, what a mixed, conglomerate mass of iniquity would be left behind! You can realize that better if you stop to consider what the Church of God has meant throughout the centuries. People often debate the question as to whether the world is better or worse than it was 1900 years ago. Some insist that the world is worse, and that it is constantly getting worse. They quote the scripture, "Evil men and seducers shall wax worse and worse, deceiving, and being deceived" (2 Tim. 3: 13). Others insist that the world is better, and they point to the millions of Christian people, to the kindliness and the interest in the poor and needy that prevail in many lands where once the vilest cruelty existed. But, in my judgment, both are wrong.

The world is no worse than it was 1900 years ago. When Scripture says that "Evil men and seducers shall wax worse and worse," it is simply telling us what has always been true, and always will be true of people who turn away from God. As men give themselves up to evil, certainly they get worse and worse as time goes on. That was always so; it is so today. Wherever you find evil men, they grow worse and worse. But the world is not worse today than it was when our blessed Lord Jesus was here. The greatest crime that has ever been committed was committed 1900 years ago in the murder of the Son of God. Now the world continues to condone that crime, and as long as it continues to reject the Lord Jesus Christ it will never get any better. Therefore the world is not getting any better. It is not improving. But, you say, think of the Christians, of the churches all over the land, of the kindliness and interest in the needy that prevail in many places. Yes, we take all that into consideration, but the question is this, "Is the *world* getting any better?" If you want to find out if the world is getting any better, you must subtract the Church. If you could imagine this scene with every Christian gone, you would have "the world," and you would find that world just as corrupt, just as vile, just as wicked as it was 1900 years ago. It is true that this globe is a much more comfortable place on which to have a home than it was 1900 years ago. We enjoy a great many inventions, and have benefited by a great many things that minister to human need and comfort that were unknown then, but these things do not change the hearts of men. Men are just as wicked with electricity, with radios, with stream-line trains, with motor-boats, with air-planes, as they were before these things were known.

In this world there is something very dear to the heart of the Son of God. He called it, "My Church." When Peter made his great declaration, "Thou art the Christ, the Son of the Living God," Jesus said, "Blessed art thou, Simon Barjona: for flesh and blood hath not revealed it unto thee, but My Father which is in heaven; and I say unto thee, That thou art Peter, and upon this rock"—the Rock that thou hast confessed—"I will build My Church; and the gates of hell shall not prevail against it" (Matt. 16: 17, 18). The Holy Spirit has likened that Church to Christ's Body, His Bride—"Christ loved the Church, and gave Himself for it; that He might sanctify and cleanse it with the washing of water by the Word" (Eph. 5: 25, 26).

The Church is looked at in two aspects. In the first place it includes all believers everywhere at any time since the day of Pentecost. Now, whether these people have intimate church relationship with others or not, they belong to "the Church which is His Body, the fulness of Him that filleth all in all" (Eph. 1:23). But the Scripture also contemplates *churches*. You read of the churches of Galatia, the churches of Judea, the seven churches of Asia, etc., and these local churches are groups of confessed believers. Not always are all of them real believers, but presumably, they all profess to be believers, and so gather together for worship, for praise, for prayer, and for Christian testimony. This has been so from the beginning. Those that "received the Word were baptized: and the same day there were added unto them about three thousand souls. And they continued stedfastly in the apostles' doctrine and fellowship, and in breaking of bread, and in prayers" (Acts 2: 41, 42). We need this fellowship, we need this outward expression of Christian testimony, and so God by His Spirit forms local churches in various places where His people gather together thus to worship Him. There are some who say, "I am a Christian and belong to the Church, the Body of Christ, and I do not need to be associated with any local body of Christians. If I could find one absolutely perfect, I would join it." But then, it would be spoiled after you got in, for you would be the first bad thing in it, because you would go in with that critical spirit of yours, and that would spoil the whole testimony. It is never contemplated in Scripture that local churches will be perfect companies of believers. From the beginning you find a great many imperfect people in local assemblies, but that is no reason why they should be disbanded. Therefore, you and I as Christians are responsible to walk in fellow-

ship with other Christians. They need us and
we need them. Some people who find it very
difficult to get along with others get a great blessing for putting up with them. The hardest thing,
if endured for Christ's sake, will bring blessing.
It drives us to our knees to self-examination,
leads us to ask ourselves, "What is the matter
with me that I find it so hard to please such
absolutely good people?" We are all just poor
sinners saved by grace, but some day we are
going to be just like the Lord Jesus Christ, and
as He is so patient with us, we can afford to be
patient one with another.

We find from this epistle that there was a
great deal in the early Church that was far from
satisfactory. We have seen the difficulties the
apostle Paul had even with his own converts. He
would go into a certain place and lead people to
Christ, and it would not be long before they
thought they knew more than he did, and some
of them, in their own estimation, became so much
holier than he that they no longer wanted to have
fellowship with him!

As he comes to the last part of the portion of
the epistle, in which he has attempted to justify
his own ministry, Paul shows us that there are
both helpers and hinderers in the Church of God.
You can settle it in your own mind as to which
you are, whether a helper or a hinderer. You

are one or the other. You are either helping the testimony, spreading the gospel, commending Christ to other people, or you are hindering, by leading people to question whether there is anything real in the salvation of which we speak.

Let us notice first of all how grace wrought in the apostle Paul. He did not like to speak of himself, but the Holy Spirit made him do so. For the fourth or fifth time he says that he is a fool as he speaks of himself, "I am become a fool in glorying; ye have compelled me: for I ought to have been commended of you." God had given him this mission and he could not think lightly of it. Because he had led them to Christ he should have been commended of them. It was like little children trying to tell a father what to do and how to behave. Not so very many months ago I was in a home and something was going on upstairs while I waited in the car. A young lady of about seventeen years of age came down the stairs, and said to me, "You must excuse me, I do get so angry. I have an awful job making Father behave!" That is the spirit of the day, and these Corinthians were trying to regulate their father in Christ.

Paul now says that he has to tell them something of the mission intrusted to him, which was not given to any other man. He says, "For in nothing am I behind the very chiefest apostles, though I be nothing." You have here a wonderful combination of the importance of the mission committed to him and of Christian humility. He would have been false to his commission had he failed to recognize the fact that he was indeed in nothing behind the very chiefest apostles. The Lord Jesus Christ had committed to him such a ministry as no other apostle had fully entered into, but he to whom this ministry was committed said, "Though I be nothing." In his first epistle to them he rebuked the Corinthians for making too much of leaders and saying, "I am of Paul, I am of Apollos, I am of Cephas," and says, "Who is Paul, and who is Apollos, but ministers by whom ye believed?" (1 Cor. 1: 12; 3: 5). But the minister is nothing, Christ is all; and so he sets the example of true Christian humility. One who would be a helper in the work of the Lord must be a humble man. God refuses to identify His name for long with those that walk in pride. "Those that walk in pride He is able to abase" (Dan. 4: 37). If we have not the mind of Christ, we will not be used of God as He would like to use us. Let us search our own hearts and see whether we are cherishing that unholy pride which goes before destruction. There is many a man of remarkable ability whom God has to put to one side because a proud, haughty spirit comes in continually to interfere with the work of the Lord. May God teach us to be lowly, and help us to "walk worthy of the Lord unto all pleasing" (Col. 1: 10).

Notice in the third place, the devotedness of this man. In verse 12 we read, "Truly the signs of an apostle were wrought among you in all patience, in signs, and wonders, and mighty deeds." The miracles he wrought proved he was divinely approved and accredited. "For what is it wherein ye were inferior to other churches, except it be that I myself was not burdensome to you? Forgive me this wrong: Behold, the third time I am ready to come to you; and I will not be burdensome to you: for I seek not yours, but you: for the children ought not to lay up for the parents, but the parents for the children." He was out in the work of the Lord and he was unequaled as a teacher and a preacher. Did he set a price upon his ministry? Did he say, "I refuse to preach, to teach, unless you pay me a certain salary"? No; he said, "I will very gladly spend and be spent for you." And when he found there was a wrong spirit among them he decided that he would take nothing from them, and all the time he was ministering to them he had received his support from other churches who sent their offerings to him. These Corinthians did not understand it, and so said, "He cannot be a real apostle or he would be taking money for his services." But he says, "The very fact that I am here to serve you freely ought to be to you the evidence that I have no selfish motive." He was an unselfish man, a devoted man, there was something so frank, so childlike, so whole-hearted about him, that it should have commended him to their love and confidence. "I will very gladly spend and be spent for you; though the more abundantly I love you, the less I be loved"—I am willing to lay myself out for you whether you think much of me or not, I am here to do you good. And yet they tried to see some hidden motive behind it all and said, "He is crafty, he is putting on this appearance of humility, he is pretending to be meek and lowly in order to have influence over us and exercise authority over us." "Nevertheless, being crafty, I caught you with guile!" Is he saying that he did this? No, he is quoting what they said about him, for they said, "He is deceitful, his apparent disinterestedness is just craft, and he is pretending to be so humble and lowly in order that he may hold us under his thumb." The apostle repudiates anything of the kind and says, "My preaching was not with enticing words of man's wisdom" (1 Cor. 2: 4). "Did I make a gain of you by any whom I sent unto you? I desired Titus, and with him I sent a brother. Did Titus make a gain of you? He had sent Titus to receive their gift for

the needy saints, and with him another to count
the money, that there might be no misunderstanding.
"Walked we not in the same spirit? walked
we not in the same steps?"—showing that our
entire service was absolutely unselfish.

Then notice, his own life was summed up in
living for others, "Again, think ye that we excuse
ourselves unto you? We speak before God in
Christ: but we do all things, dearly beloved, for
your edifying." Although you and I are far from
being apostles, yet we can all be characterized by
the same spirit of humility, of devotedness to
Christ, of unselfish service for others.

Now look at the contrast. See what has been
manifested in these Corinthians as this evil spirit
of fault-finding took hold on them. "I fear, lest,
when I come, I shall not find you such as I would,
and that I shall be found unto you such as ye
would not: lest there be debates, envyings,
wraths, strifes, backbitings, whisperings, swellings,
tumults." Let us face this passage honestly,
and see whether we have fallen under the power
of any of these unholy things. "Lest there be
debates." What does that mean? It is what you
so often see when two or three people get to
fussing about this and that. What a childish
spirit this is, and yet how it hurts the work of
the Lord. And then in the second place, "envyings."
How few people there are who can re-

joice in what others are accomplishing, who can
delight to see others honored and recognized. In
the third place, "wrath," for envy cherished leads
to wrath. And how easy it is to be censorious
and bitter. That which begins in a small fault-
finding way, if not judged, soon degenerates into
positive ill-will toward others. And then, "strife."
How often there is strife between God's people.
"Backbitings." You know the sister who comes
to you and says, "Did you hear about Brother
So-and-So?"

"No."

"Well, I don't know that I ought to tell you."

"Oh, yes, do."

"Well, it is really awful."

And just then Brother So-and-So walks in the
door, and the sisters say, "Why, how do you do?
We were just talking of you. Speak of an angel,
and he's sure to appear!" It isn't always the
sisters who do this. It is often the brothers too.

Miserable hypocrites! Backbiting, saying
things behind the back that they would never
dare to say to the face! If every time someone
said something evil or unkind behind another's
back the other person would say, "Is that so?
Well, let us go and talk to him about it," this
thing would soon be stopped. Then, "whisperings." A meeting breaks up, and a little group
over here is whispering and fault-finding, and

there a group is together whispering and complaining. Judge whether you have ever been guilty of anything of the kind. "Swellings." I do not recall what that Greek word is, but this word always makes me think of a bull-frog sitting on a log puffing, puffing, puffing. Throw a stone at him, and he goes down to a very small size. And then, "tumults." How many churches have been wrecked when at last these evil things have resulted in tumults, internal troubles that divide and destroy the work. We can be very grateful to God that through the Holy Spirit He has indicated these dangerous things so that we can avoid them and be helpers instead of hinderers.

Why did they find fault with the apostle Paul? He had to be very strict about some wicked things that had been tolerated by some people in the church at Corinth, and he says, "Lest, when I come again, my God will humble me among you, and that I shall bewail many which have sinned already, and have not repented of the uncleanness and fornication and lasciviousness which they have committed." Some of these people had fallen into unclean and unholy things, and in order to cover up their own pollution they were finding fault with Christ's servant because of his faithfulness. That is always the effect of sin. Hidden sin in the life will result in unfair criticism of the servants of God who stand against things of that kind and seek to lift up a standard of holiness and purity.

And so, may we face the question, Am I a hinderer or a helper? God has committed to His Church the business of making known the gospel of His grace to a lost world. I want by His help to carry it on and not to hinder. May God impress on our hearts the importance of devoted living for the blessing of others.

CRUCIFIED THROUGH WEAKNESS

✓ ✓ ✓

"This is the third time I am coming to you. In the mouth of two or three witnesses shall every word be established. I told you before, and foretell you, as if I were present, the second time; and being absent now I write to them which heretofore have sinned, and to all other, that, if I come again, I will not spare: since ye seek a proof of Christ speaking in me, which to you-ward is not weak, but is mighty in you. For though He was crucified through weakness, yet He liveth by the power of God. For we also are weak in Him, but we shall live with Him by the power of God toward you. Examine yourselves, whether ye be in the faith; prove your own selves. Know ye not your own selves, how that Jesus Christ is in you, except ye be reprobates? But I trust that ye shall know that we are not reprobates. Now I pray to God that ye do no evil; not that we should appear approved, but that ye should do that which is honest, though we be as reprobates. For we can do nothing against the truth but for the truth. For we are glad, when we are weak, and ye are strong: and this also we wish, even your perfection. Therefore I write these things being absent, lest being present I should use sharpness, according to the power which the Lord hath given me to edification, and not to destruction. Finally, brethren, farewell. Be perfect, be of good comfort, be of one mind, live in peace; and the God of love and peace shall be with you. Greet one another with an holy kiss. All the saints salute you. The grace of the Lord Jesus Christ, and the love of God, and the communion of the Holy Ghost, be with you all. Amen." (2 Cor. 13: 1-14).

THIS last chapter may really be divided into two parts, and yet they are so intimately connected that I want to discuss it all at the same time. The apostle, you remember, had told these Corinthians on two previous occasions that he had been arranging to come to see them, but certain circumstances hindered. Just what forms these circumstances took we are not told, but he was unable to come; and because he had not kept his partial promise there were those who accused him of lightness, of levity, in promising things which he did not do. Others declared there was a very good reason why he did not come. They said, "He has charged us with certain things, which he is taking for granted are true, and he does not dare to come and face us about them." And he said, "I am coming, the third time I am coming, and when I come, in the mouth of two or three witnesses every word will be established. I have written you beforehand of behavior contrary to Christian principles. All I have heard will be fully substantiated, and I hope when I get there I will find you really repentant of these evil things and not condoning them." "I told you before, and foretell you, as if I were present, the second time; and being absent now I write to them which heretofore have sinned, and to all other, that, if I come again, I will not spare." He did not like to come. He says on one occasion,

"To spare you I refrained from coming," but he could not put it off; he would come to them and deal with those things face to face. Unholiness is incompatible with the testimony of the Church of God, which is the temple of the living God. "Holiness becometh Thine house, O Lord, forever." And if those who are linked up with others in Christian fellowship are living unholy lives, they should be put away from the assembly, but if they repent they are to be restored to full communion.

In replying again to the suggestion that Paul was not a real apostle, he says, "If you seek a proof of Christ living in me, examine yourselves." Now if you take this fifth verse out of its connection you lose the meaning of it. Many people take it, as though he meant that we are to examine ourselves to see if we are real Christians, but that is not what Paul was saying. They questioned his apostleship, whether the Spirit of God was in his ministry. If you will look at everything after "speaking in me," verse three down through verse four, as parenthetical, then you get his exact meaning. "Since ye seek a proof of Christ speaking in me, examine yourselves." In other words, he is saying, "Are you Christians? How did you become Christians? Was it not through my ministry? Well, then God was working in me. If you are hypocrites, if you are not real

Christians, then Christ did not work in me. If you are real Christians, if you have the assurance that you are the children of God, you received that as a result of the testimony that I brought to you at Corinth. Therefore you ought to be the last people in the world to question whether Christ wrought through me."

I suppose we are all indebted to some servant of Christ for our present knowledge of the truth. If we are not living in a godly manner, it is reflecting discredit on the one who brought us to Christ. If we want to bring credit to our fathers and mothers in Christ, then we should live to the glory of God. There are certain things that the world looks upon as its own, and I am here to represent my Father, and I do not want to bring discredit on my Father's name. The Book says, "Love not the world, neither the things that are in the world. If any man love the world, the love of the Father is not in him. For all that is in the world, the lust of the flesh, and the lust of the eyes, and the pride of life, is not of the Father, but is of the world. And the world passeth away, and the lust thereof: but he that doeth the will of God abideth forever." Oh, I wish that we as Christians might ever keep that in mind! We are here in the world to represent our Father and to represent our Saviour, and men can but get their conception of God and of Christ, our blessed

Lord, through us. We may well examine ourselves, therefore, and see if we are so behaving as to bring glory to our Lord Jesus Christ.

Let us now go back and look at the parenthesis. Paul turns aside and exclaims concerning his ministry, "Which to you-ward is not weak, but is mighty in you. For though He was crucified through weakness, yet He liveth by the power of God. For we also are weak in Him, but we shall live with Him by the power of God toward you." This is the parenthesis. Now notice how solemnly he brings before us the humiliation Christ endured for our redemption, which we are in a measure called to share. "He was crucified through weakness." What does that mean? Does it mean He was so weak in Himself that He was unable to resist His foes? Or was He simply the victim of circumstances? Oh, no. The preposition translated "through" here is generally rendered "in." He was crucified in weakness, but He liveth again in the power of God. It simply means this: He chose to become a Man for our redemption. He chose to be made "a little lower than the angels for the suffering of death." He who was higher than the highest "did not count it (equality with God) a thing to be grasped," but He emptied Himself of the glory He had before the world was, and "being found in fashion as a man, He humbled Himself and became obedient unto death, and such a death, that of the cross." In this sense He was crucified through weakness. As excarnate God He could never have died for our sin. But He chose to become incarnate. He chose to become a man, and to be subject to hunger and thirst and weariness and every sinless infirmity of mankind, and He chose not to resist His foes. He allowed Himself to be spat upon, to be beaten, to be crowned with thorns. "I gave My back to the smiters and My cheek to them that plucked off the hair: I hid not My face from shame and spitting." He chose to be "despised and rejected of men; a man of sorrows, and acquainted with grief." It was His own desire thus to give Himself a ransom for all, and so we read in his first epistle (chap. 1:21-25): "After that in the wisdom of God the world by wisdom knew not God, it pleased God by the foolishness of preaching to save them that believe. For the Jews require a sign, and the Greeks seek after wisdom; but we preach Christ crucified, unto the Jews a stumbling-block, and unto the Greeks foolishness; but unto them which are called, both Jews and Greeks, Christ the power of God and the wisdom of God." Now listen: "Because the foolishness of God is wiser than men; and the weakness of God is stronger than men." Think of these two expressions: First, "The foolishness of God;" what does it mean? It is really, "the simplicity of God." It means that God's wondrous plan of redemption through the cross is foolishness to the philosopher, the man of this world; but the Scripture says, "The foolishness of God is wiser than men." And, second, "The weakness of God;" what does that imply? God becoming Man, God submitting to the agony and shame of the cross, God in Christ bleeding, suffering, dying for our redemption. "The weakness of God is stronger than men." God could do through the cross what He never could do apart from the cross. Oh, the miracles that have been wrought through the cross all down the centuries! Do you know of anything else that can change the heart of a hard, cruel and godless man, transform him and make a new creature of him?

A minister tells how on one occasion in New Guinea, where perhaps less than a score of years before the heathen were utterly wrapped in darkness, through a testimony carried on there by faithful witnesses the people were gathered reverently at the table of the Lord, and here sat a missionary of the cross. Beside him sat an elder of the native church. The minister recognized in this elder the son of a man who had eaten the missionary father of the son sitting there. The son of the martyred missionary and the son of the man who had killed him, were both remembering the Lord Jesus as the Saviour of mankind. Do you know of anything that can bind hearts together like this?

You recall the story of Kayarnak, the first convert of the Moravian missionaries in Greenland. When they went to that country and found the people so steeped in iniquity, they said, "They will never understand the gospel. These people are drunkards, gluttons, they are adulterers, they are living the vilest of lives. They won't understand the grace of God, they will take it as a license for sin." So the Moravian missionaries drilled into the hearts and minds of that people God's holy law. They said they had to do it to create a conscience in the Esquimoux. But the results were nil. No man had ever sought out a missionary for conference about his soul. They listened to the messages and went back and lived their wicked lives again. And then Hans Egede came, his heart burning with love for that people. He had left wealth and honor to sacrifice himself for those unspeakably vile Greenlanders. It was announced he would speak in a certain neighborhood on a Lord's Day. They crowded into a small lodge holding 200 to 300 people. It was a poor affair, built up from pieces of old wrecked ships. There they sat. Hans Egede stood up and preached and, for the first time in the history of Greenland, told the story of the cross. Tenderly, lovingly, with a heart that had itself been broken by the power of the cross, he told of the One who had suffered and bled for the redemption of sinners. It took an hour or two to tell his story, and when he finished Kayarnak, a young chief, who had been listening eagerly as the gospel was proclaimed, sprang forward and cried, "Missionaries, why did you not tell us this before? You have been with us a year, and you never told us before. You told us of a God who created a world, and it did not make us hate our sin. You told us of a God who gave His holy law. We learned the ten commandments, and we went out and got drunk again, but today you have told us how our sins broke the heart of God and He came to redeem us from our sins. Missionary, Kayarnak cannot sin against love like that. From now on Kayarnak will be a Christian." And Kayarnak became the outstanding Christian testimony for years in Greenland. "The weakness of God is stronger than men." We have sometimes tried to reason people into salvation, forgetting that our commission is to preach His Word, to preach Christ. Paul says, "We preach Christ crucified, the power and wisdom of God." He was crucified in weakness. Let us never forget that. My sin put Him there; your sin put Him there. What do I mean? You say, "We are Christians; do you mean the sins we committed before we were

saved?" I mean the sin that you committed last
night, that sin nailed the Son of God to the
cross; that sin that you have been meditating
today, that sin put God on the cross.   All the
sins that you and I have committed, of thought,
of word and of deed, God saw them all, and for
all of them the Son of God suffered, and if you
deliberately walk out and commit sin you are sinning against the cross of Christ. You cannot live
like the world without trampling on the Son of
God. You cannot go on in things that His Book
condemns without deliberately piercing, as it
were, the side of the Son of God afresh.

And yet it is not a dead Christ that we serve.
He liveth by the power of God and He said, "Because I live, ye shall live also." We have a living
Christ and He desires us to walk in His steps, to
live in separation from the world. His people
are not of the world, and that is one reason why
they will never be understood by the world. You
cannot walk as He walked and please the world;
it is impossible. He says, "Ye are not of the
world, even as I am not of the world. If ye were
of the world, the world would love his own." Oh,
the absurdity—shall I say—or the fanaticism of
imagining that you can be a consistent Christian
and yet live like the world. It is folly of the
worst kind. If you are saved through the Christ
that the world rejected, you take Him as your

Lord and seek to live the kind of life He lived. Do you want to know what it was? Turn back to the four Gospels and see.

"Now I pray to God that ye do no evil; not that we should appear approved, but that ye should do that which is honest, though we be as reprobates." It is a dishonest thing to profess to serve Christ and not yield your life to His control. If those Corinthians were really Christians, then the gospel that Paul preached had been believed, and if believed it would show through the life. The truth proclaimed goes on from victory to victory. Note the unselfishness of this man Paul: "We are glad when we are weak and ye are strong." That is not the world's way. We should be willing to take the lowest place. You see, Paul never sees the saints as perfect in the body. "Not as though I had already attained, either were already perfect: but I follow after, if that I may lay hold of that for which also I have been laid hold of by Christ Jesus." But he is seeking the perfection of the saints, going on to this perfect, fully-developed Christian character. That only comes as we walk in fellowship with Christ.

"Therefore I write these things being absent, lest being present I should use sharpness." He does not want to say some stern things that very much needed to be said. "According to the power which the Lord hath given me to edification, and not to destruction."

And then comes the conclusion of his epistle: "Finally, brethren, farewell. Be perfect." I desire your perfection. Literally, be perfected, by continual growth. "Be of good comfort." Cheer up. "Be of one mind, live in peace." I think one thing that brings great distress and hindrance to the work of the Lord is when believers speak so unkindly of others. Let us learn to speak well of our brethren in Christ. "Live in peace; and the God of love and peace shall be with you." "Greet one another with an holy kiss." Do not put the emphasis on "kiss." He is not saying that you are to greet people with a kiss. "Greet one another with a *holy* kiss. That is where you put the emphasis. Greet one another with a holy hand-shake. It is a very unholy hand-shake if on meeting a brother we say, "Well, my dear brother, how do you do?" and then turn away and say, "I have no use for him." That is a very unholy hand-shake. Judas kissed the Lord and it was an unholy kiss; it was a kiss of hypocrisy. "All the saints salute you."

And now we have that well-known benediction that has been heard ten million times since Paul wrote it: "The grace of the Lord Jesus Christ, and the love of God, and the communion of the Holy Ghost, be with you all. Amen."

In these words we have epitomised for us the outstanding doctrines of the Christian faith. The truth of the Holy Trinity is here presented as definitely as in Matt. 28: 19. The grace of the Son, the love of the Father, and the fellowship of the Spirit, include every blessing that is ours through the infinite mercy of God: grace to cover all our sins, and to strengthen us for every conflict; love to cheer and sustain our hearts in every trial; and a hallowed fellowship that gives us to enter into and enjoy our rich inheritance in Christ!